IMAGES
of America

AROUND
DRIPPING SPRINGS

By the time this 1885 amended layout of Dripping Springs was filed by local merchant and land speculator W.T. Chapman, the town was fairly bustling. The *San Marcos Free Press* reported an estimated $100,000 worth of business changing hands in Dripping Springs, with a population of approximately 300. Chapman filed several updates to his original 12-block layout between 1881 and 1885. (Drane & Associates.)

ON THE COVER: Annie Young Harris is pictured in 1889 with her parents and children. The adults are, from left to right, Robert S. Young, his wife, Sarah Jane, and their daughter Annie. Annie's children are, from left to right, Ellen Harris, Oscar Harris, and Jennie Harris. Annie and her husband, Samuel L. Harris, moved the family to the Dripping Springs area in the late 1800s and temporarily lived in this military surplus tent (No. 20) while building their home. Descendants of little Jennie Harris, who grew up to marry H. Wiley Roberts, continue to live in the area today. (Pam Roberts McAfee.)

IMAGES
of America

AROUND
DRIPPING SPRINGS

L.M. Freeman
Foreword by Carl Waits

ARCADIA
PUBLISHING

Published by Arcadia Publishing
Charleston, South Carolina

Library of Congress Control Number: 2011930417

For all general information, please contact Arcadia Publishing:
Telephone 843-853-2070
Fax 843-853-0044
E-mail sales@arcadiapublishing.com
For customer service and orders:
Toll-Free 1-888-313-2665

Visit us on the Internet at www.arcadiapublishing.com

CONTENTS

FOREWORD

While working on my book about the history of Dripping Springs, the importance of having additional pictures to make the information come alive became clear. I am delighted that *Around Dripping Springs* will bring together so many more photographs from collections carefully and lovingly preserved by generations of local families.

These historic images of Dripping Springs, Driftwood, and Henly are better than thousands of words to help tell the stories of people, places, and events that have shaped the area. These stories-through-pictures can also help provide guidance and insights for the future. I believe that when the residents of a community realize what has been accomplished in the past, it is easier to face what lies ahead.

I know *Around Dripping Springs* will be enjoyed by old-timers and newcomers alike. As a former history teacher, I hope this book becomes another way for everyone to learn more about the town of Dripping Springs and surrounding areas, whether they are just passing through or decide—like so many others have before them—to call "Dripping" home.

—Carl Waits
author of *The Complete History of Dripping Springs, Texas and the P.A. Smith Survey*

ACKNOWLEDGMENTS

I have been an avid reader of all kinds of books since childhood. I always try to read the author's acknowledgments and have wondered if it would be difficult to write. Now I can say that I know it is.

As straightforwardly as possible, I would like to say to the many local residents who so freely contributed to this project and asked nothing in return: Thank you! Humbly, abundantly, since rely—thank you! Thank you for finding and sharing your family photograph collections, thank you for entrusting your priceless pictures into my care, thank you for welcoming a complete stranger into your homes and into your histories, thank you for your hospitality and friendship so easily extended, thank you for your interest in me and my family, and thank you for being so proud of your heritage and willing to passionately share it so others might come to love and appreciate this area, too. Each one of you has made this newcomer feel welcome and proud to be your neighbor. You know who you are, but this is the part where I get to name names, so my heartfelt appreciation goes specifically to Travis Garnett, Lila Gillespie, Peggy Montgomery, Pam & Scott McAfee; Pam, Courtney, Jamye, Rosemary, and Brenda at Print Plus; J. Marie Bassett, Marianne Simmons, Charlie Haydon, Grady Moore, Clarence Cobb, Louise Hall, Sandra Coe, Clara Gravell, Scott Roberts, Maile Roberts, Carolyn Gully, Johnny Hudson, George Mading, David Crenshaw, June McCarty, Sally Gravenor, Dr. Dennis Cannon, Lawrence & Patty Coffee, Barbara Jones, Mt. Horeb Baptist Church, Patsy Hurlbut, Wanda Glass, H.C. Carter, Clay Dement, Ross S. Jennings, Janie Botkin, Carl Waits, Pat Jones, Dave & Anita Drane, Claireen & Doyle Fellers, Kathryn Chandler, Lance Armstrong Foundation, City of Dripping Springs, Dripping Springs Chamber of Commerce Visitor's Center, Dr. Pound Historical Farmstead Museum, Dripping Springs Historic Preservation Commission, Hays County Historical Commission, and Henly Homecoming.

Even closer to home, my husband and our three daughters went above and beyond to provide plenty of cheer, patience, support, encouragement, candy, coffee, and smiles throughout this experience, for which I am grateful. I also had the privilege to work with "dream" Arcadia acquisitions editor, Lauren Hummer, whose professionalism, knowledgeable guidance, responsiveness, and humor resuscitated me more than once along the way. Thanks for all you do, Lauren!

INTRODUCTION

One of these days, I will actually buy the bumper sticker that declares, "I wasn't born in Texas, but I got here as fast as I could!" When my family and I moved to the Dripping Springs area, it was my third time moving to Texas. It came as no surprise that I fell in love all over again with the Lone Star State, its spirited people, and its pioneering history. What did surprise me was the richness of this area's history. Not long after arriving, our youngest daughter was assigned a middle school project to explore historic sites in the area, and I found myself wanting to learn more. That is when a school project turned into a book project.

There are three main themes clearly woven into the fabric of the area's history: a high standard of education from the start, entrepreneurial leadership and innovation, and equality in the form of community support for everyone. By and large, the many generations of families—black, white, native, and Hispanic—who have lived and died here over nearly 200 years have helped each other to overcome tremendous odds to educate themselves and their children, and to creatively and consistently carve out a living for their families. It seems that people who work hard, keep their word, help their neighbors, and respect the local culture are welcome and will get back as good as they give. In short, the story of the Dripping Springs area is a story of the American Dream.

I have enjoyed learning about the many characters, changes, and challenges that have molded Dripping Springs, Henly, and Driftwood into the resilient yet charming communities they remain today. I hope this pictorial history will help to inspire and motivate old-timers and newcomers alike to continue to preserve, honor, and respect the area's deeply rooted pioneering spirit and long-standing commitments to community, education, faith, prosperity, and freedom. For anyone already well-acquainted with local history, it will be the personal stories and photographs that bring a fresh view of familiar names and places. For those who are new to the area, this pictorial history will provide a fascinating up close and personal look at the faces and families that have defined Drippings Springs since before Texas got its star.

Many historic events, dates, and people have had to be omitted due to formatting and length requirements. Noticeably absent are historic photographs and stories from local Hispanic families. Unfortunately, I was unable to obtain material to make these references. However, many other residents with deep family roots have said of their Hispanic neighbors that they, too, worked shoulder-to-shoulder, shared each other's burdens, celebrated each others' joys, and relied on one another to help carve out a life for all of their families.

For a more detailed and comprehensive history of Dripping Springs, a great resource is *The Complete History of Dripping Springs Texas* and the *P.A. Smith Survey* by local resident and former history teacher Carl Waits. Two others are *Driftwood Heritage: The History of Driftwood, Texas* by resident Minnie Lea Rogers, and *Clear Springs and Limestone Ledges: A History of San Marcos and Hays County* by the Hays County Historical Commission. The Dripping Springs Community Library also houses a collection of essays and recorded interviews for use on-site.

One

NATIVES AND NEWCOMERS

The original road between Austin and Dripping Springs runs parallel to today's Highway 290. Wide in places and just a narrow wagon-wheel track in others, the old dirt road runs on top of a ridge alongside 290 West, passing beneath the base of the town's landmark "Gateway to the Hill Country" water tower. The commute to Austin now takes about 30 minutes. The trip with a team and wagon took the better part of a day on the old road.

The Tonkawa Indians were the first recorded inhabitants of the Dripping Springs area. As nomadic hunter-gatherers, they shared many traits with neighboring Texas tribes. But the Tonkawa—whose name means "they all stay together"—were also despised because of belief that they gained strength from the flesh of their enemies through the practice of ritualistic cannibalism. The isolated Tonkawa began serving as scouts for Anglo settlers and soldiers battling Comanches and Apaches. The Tonkawa allied themselves as scouts with the Texans against the Comanche and Apache; they also fought alongside Texas Rangers for independence from Mexico and sided with the Confederacy during the Civil War. In 1857, Chief Grant Richards and his wife, Winnie, (pictured) accompanied the Tonkawa to Oklahoma. Their allegiance to the Texans and their reputation as cannibals cost them dearly among reservation Indians. In 1862, half the tribe was massacred by pro-Union Indian tribes. By 1921, only 34 Tonkawa remained in Oklahoma, but the population has slowly recovered. Nearly 200 Tonkawa were reported on reservation lands in the late 1990s.

The granite dome of Enchanted Rock near Fredericksburg got its name from the local Indians—including the Tonkawa—who believed flickering ghost fires could be seen on top of the rock at night. Enduring legends abound about this popular hiking and camping destination, now managed by Texas Parks and Wildlife. One tale tells of an Anglo woman kidnapped by Indians; she allegedly escaped and lived on top of Enchanted Rock, where her screams were said to be heard at night. According to the Texas State Historical Association, local Comanche and Tonkawa feared and revered Enchanted Rock, and may have offered sacrifices at its base.

"Where the Tonkawa once prowled, the cool, clear waters of the Edwards Aquifer burst forth along this brook and dripped musically from the limestone overhead." So begins the inscription written by historian Robert E. Shelton on the granite monument to "The Dripping Springs." Water no longer bursts forth here, but it still flows slowly among the ferns beneath the Mercer Street overpass.

Indiana "Nannie" Moss was among the first of the Anglo newcomers to the area and is credited with naming the town Dripping Springs after the local Indian watering hole. Nannie and her husband, John Moss, are among three families credited with founding Dripping Springs. The other two families are Joseph and Sarah Pound (Nannie's sister) and John and Malvina Wallace. The Pounds and the Mosses may have left Mississippi together in the fall of 1853, arriving in early 1854, while the Wallaces may have come directly from Kentucky. Regardless of when they all arrived, their settlement took root; and by 1857, a post office was established with John Moss as postmaster. The little town needed a name. It is commonly believed Moss's wife, Nannie, suggested the name Dripping Springs. By 1860, John and Nannie Moss had moved to nearby Blanco County. (Dr. Pound Historical Farmstead Museum.)

The first settler known to purchase land that included the Dripping Springs area was Willis Fawcett. Fawcett's half league of land was purchased in the fall of 1853, but he was not the first to be drawn to the abundance of water and wood found along Onion Creek. Originally named Sheep Tick by the Spanish, the creek was renamed by early Texas settlers in Stephen F. Austin's "Little Colony" for the wild onions growing in abundance at the mouth of the stream. Today, this cypress stump on Onion Creek in Driftwood bears mute testimony to the pioneers' lust for lumber. According to the book *Driftwood Heritage*, by Minnie Lea Rogers, "many thousands of bundles of cypress shingles were made (in Driftwood) and sold in Austin." Shingles were so valuable they were even used to purchase land. Fortunately, many tall and beautiful cypress trees stand intact today along Onion Creek.

Dr. Joseph M. Pound is the frontrunner for the title of Founding Father of Dripping Springs. After earning a degree in medicine at the University of Louisville in Kentucky, Dr. Pound married Sarah Dunbiben Ward in Mississippi, in 1853. The newlyweds struck out for Texas that same year, arriving in early 1854, where they soon settled the town of Dripping Springs with the newly arrived Wallace and Moss families. All three families are known to have brought slaves with them. (Dr. Pound Historical Farmstead Museum.)

Dr. Joseph Pound and his new bride, Sarah, first lived in the Henly area when they arrived in January 1854. According to *Clear Springs and Limestone Ledges: A History of San Marcos and Hays County*, the area got its name from a rancher named Henly, who acquired a large piece of land in the vicinity. Meanwhile, settler John Moss bought land from the neighboring P.A. Smith Survey that same month. John Wallace also bought acreage, possibly in June of that year. By December 1854, Dr. Pound had purchased 700 acres just north of the Wallace property. Out of these three homesteads sprang the community of Dripping Springs. The hamlet of Henly also took root during these pioneering years. Rubble from "old Henly" can still be seen along Route 165.

Posing in this 1912 Pound family photograph are, from left to right, granddaughter Marguerite Cavett Hammack, Sarah Pound, Dr. Joseph Pound, and granddaughter Mittie Lou "Birdie" Walters. By the time this photograph was taken, the house had undergone several expansions from the original log cabin. Early protection from Indian raids and severe weather was provided by a rock-walled cellar. An innovative water cistern built into a kitchen wall enabled water to be drawn from inside through a window. The house also served as a hospital. Pound family descendants occupied the home until 1983 before donating the house and property to the City of Dripping Springs for a museum. The restored Dr. Pound Historical Farmstead Museum at Founder's Park is now open to the public. Volunteers from the community help educate the public and maintain the property. (Dr. Pound Historical Farmstead Museum.)

The Pound women survived hardships and thrived with their families, as can be seen from these four generations of Pound women. From left to right are Dr. Pound's wife, Sarah; their first child, Indiana Adelia Pound Stephenson; Indiana's daughter Carrie May Stephenson Watson; and Carrie's daughter Indiana Watson. The Pounds' seventh child, Georgia Pound Cavett, described growing up on the farmstead in a recorded audio interview toward the end of her near 100-year lifespan. "Miss Georgia" told how the Indians did not bother the family because her father was a "medicine man." She also described a horse raid one night. When Dr. Pound returned from treating a patient, he put his overheated horse "on the porch and covered him." In the morning, it was the only horse left. The Indians had "made a raid and drove all the rest of them away," including the neighbors' horses. (Dr. Pound Historical Farmstead Museum.)

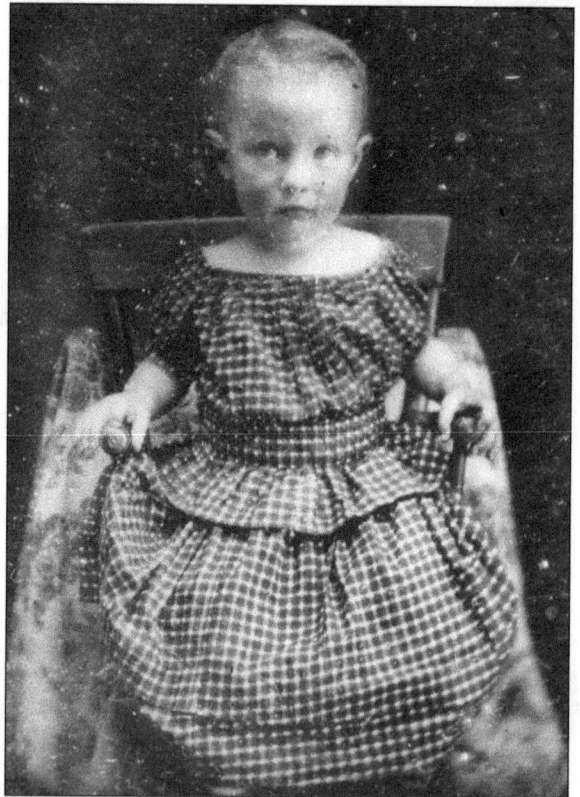

This rare daguerreotype depicts a child who may be Olive Allen Pound, the founding couple's third child. Olive was born when her mother, Sarah, was 20 years old. Olive died just three years later. It has been speculated that she looks to be seated in some type of "special chair," indicating the possibility of an illness or disability that even her father's medical skills could not heal. (Dr. Pound Historical Farmstead Museum.)

Dr. and Mrs. Pound were married 61 years, had nine children together, and lived in Dripping Springs into their 80s. The Pounds made numerous civic contributions to the area in their lifetimes by providing medical care, supporting efforts for education and commerce, and assisting military veterans and their families. Dr. Pound was also a prominent Mason when the local lodge was organized. The Masons state they are committed to education, medicine, and civic improvement. (Scott McAfee.)

Atop Wallace Mountain—the elevated landmark across Highway 290 from the big water tower—lies one of the area's oldest cemeteries. Dr. Joseph Pound and his wife, Sarah, were laid to rest here along with some of their children and descendants, as well nearly 200 other prominent residents of the area. The story goes that Wallace Mountain Cemetery came into being in the 1860s, when a family passing through lost their eight-year-old daughter. John Wallace supposedly offered a burial site on top of the mountain. Whether or not Wallace owned the land has been questioned. The property was later purchased by local merchants A.L. Davis and W.T. Chapman. When they resold it in the late 1880s, one acre was set aside for the community cemetery, which now sits on private land.

Dripping Springs founder Dr. Joseph Pound is memorialized by no less than three monuments in the Wallace Mountain Cemetery. The old stone pictured here does not detail his contributions and accomplishments. A nearby Masonic headstone acknowledges Dr. Pound's civic service. A third stone monument honors his service as a surgeon in the Civil War. In the book *Eighty Years Under the Stars and Bars: 100 Confederate Soldiers I Have Known*, it is written that Dr. Pound's "whole life was dedicated to the service of his fellow men." (Scott McAfee.)

Whether a comrade during the Civil War or a neighbor during peacetime, Dr. Pound was known as a faithful friend to many. Although no longer in regular use, this old gate still stands between the Pound and former Wallace properties. Dr. Pound reportedly had the gate installed to facilitate the families' frequent visits back and forth. The gate is located at the southeast corner of the Dr. Pound Historical Farmstead Museum grounds.

Beyond Dr. Pound's good-neighbor gate lay John and Malvina Wallace's homestead. John Lee Wallace was a distant relative of Confederate general Robert E. Lee. Local historian and writer J. Marie Bassett reports that John Wallace and Robert E. Lee were "fourth cousins, twice over" on John's mother's side. General Lee reportedly visited relatives in the area—including the Wallaces—while serving as commander of a US cavalry regiment in Texas. John and Malvina Wallace were married more than 50 years and had 11 children, although it is believed the first four or possibly five of those children died in Kentucky before the couple moved to Texas. These ruins are the remains of the Wallaces' outbuildings and house in Dripping Springs, all destroyed by fire in 1953.

Another view of the Wallace homestead rubble shows how close the ruins lie to Highway 290. Almost directly across the highway stands the H-E-B grocery store, built in 2010.

Founders John and Malvina Wallace operated a stage stop at one point. This rebuilt corral on the property along Highway 290 served as a pen for stagecoach horses. The stage corral is now located on private property, but the chain-link enclosure can still be seen from Highway 290.

John Wallace also served as a postmaster from his home in Dripping Springs—but not for the United States of America. He was appointed postmaster for the Confederate States of America in 1861. Wallace remained the Confederate postmaster for Dripping Springs throughout the war. When the South was defeated, so were Wallace's chances for serving as a United States government postmaster because of his service to the Confederacy. (Scott McAfee.)

At the base of Wallace Mountain, the Wallace Family Cemetery is believed to have been established after a family member died and heavy rain and mud prevented the funeral wagon from getting up the hill. According to the Hays County Historical Society, John and Malvina Wallace's 11th and last child, John Lee, died in 1869, at age 11 months. Three graves—including the infant John Lee's—occupy the chain-link-fenced enclosure, which received a state historical marker medallion in 2002. The tiny cemetery now sits on private property just a few feet from the shoulder of Highway 290 East, but it is often hidden from sight by overgrowth.

This marker indicates the foot of the resting place for founders John and Malvina Wallace's daughter Mattie Wallace Seal. Mattie was the second family member to be buried in the little Wallace Family Cemetery plot at the base of Wallace Mountain. She died in 1885 at age 22, survived by her husband, Charles Seal, and three-year-old daughter Pauline. (Scott McAfee.)

How many newcomers to the Dripping Springs area realize they are buzzing by the resting places along Highway 290 of members of the pioneer families who made it possible for today's residents to live here and enjoy all the area has to offer? (Scott McAfee.)

Two

FOUNDERS AND FARMERS

This marker at the gravesite of John Morris (1834–1910) in Driftwood Cemetery indicates he received a land grant from the newly liberated Republic of Texas and may have fought for Texas independence. Other markers show Morris later served as a Confederate soldier and a Mason. Numerous graves throughout Driftwood, Henly, and Dripping Springs display similar activities of local residents who came from other states and countries to settle the area.

The *San Marcos Free Press* stated in 1878 that Dripping Springs was along the Austin-Fredericksburg Road and was "an attractive region with good land, fine range, wild game and easy living." Of course, today's roads around Dripping Springs did not exist for the founders and farmers who came to help tame the beautiful but rugged terrain. It is not always clear what attracted them from their homes throughout the southern and eastern United States. Other farmers and settlers who arrived from Europe often walked their way up from the Gulf coast with their families and belongings, many also driving herds of livestock. Whether they came from Georgia or Germany, settlers to the area brought their knowledge of farming and their determination to carve out a life by whatever means of subsistence and fortune they could find or create.

The Texas county of Hays grew from a population of 387 in 1850 to 2,126 by 1860. Some passed through before returning to settle. This migrant family, the Moores, traveled by wagon throughout the area as they followed the cotton crops from Comanche to the north down to Fredericksburg and areas to the south. This picture was taken near Bell Mountain, between Llano and Fredericksburg. The tall young man in the center is 17-year-old son S.J. Moore, who settled in Dripping Springs with his own family many years afterward. Three generations of Moores went on to serve on the local school board. (Grady Moore.)

The Combs family is pictured here in the early 1900s, doing what Texas landowners still must do to occupy their land: drilling a well for water. Punching through the limestone and rock layers beneath most of Central Texas is no easy task. By the time the Combs family set about drilling this well, it appears they had the help of the machinery seen in the background. This property was actually north of Dripping Springs, in what became the Teck common school area and is now highly developed as the Lakeway community. Combs family descendants eventually moved south to a ranch on Creek Road in Dripping Springs. (Grady Moore.)

A member of the Wiley Roberts family celebrates water on their property with a picture-worthy wave. The abundance of water in underground aquifers throughout the area has always been one of the primary assurances of survival for settlers and newcomers. Pieces of the cistern pictured here remain near the entrance gate to the Rockin' P Ranch in Driftwood, still owned by a Roberts descendant. Wiley Roberts and his wife, Jennie, lived on this property until their deaths. (Pam Roberts McAfee.)

Working together, families carved out homesteads on large-acreage tracts. Wood for building was plentiful, and water was abundant, but the hard work of every adult, child, and animal was required. Area founders and the farmers industriously cultivated the land and coaxed whatever crops they could from the rocky and often thin soil. Pictured are Wiley and Jennie Roberts along with their niece Francis Irene Roberts on their Driftwood farm, which was just over 160 acres. (Pam Roberts McAfee.)

Wiley Roberts bought a small herd of cattle—also known as beeves—with the Rockin' P brand from Charles P. Harris. The brand followed the cattle, which gave the Roberts place its name. Wiley married Jennie Harris. Jennie is the little girl in the cover photograph, pictured there with her grandparents. The woman in this 1906 photograph is one of Jennie's three sisters. (Pam Roberts McAfee.)

Scratching out a living like their flock of chickens, the Jennings family learned to successfully subsist in the Mount Gainor area of Dripping Springs. The Jennings were among the first settlers in Mount Gainor, which grew relatively quickly, attracting several large families and eventually boasting a church, school, mill, and store. (K. Cannon and Berkley families.)

Not long after farming settlements took root in the area, the Civil War swept up most of the men to fight for the Confederacy. Many survivors returned and picked up where they left off. The war had forged a permanent bond of brotherhood between them that would not be broken in peacetime. Confederate veteran Capt. M.L. Reed, of Henly, was elected the first commander of Camp Ben McCulloch—a reunion campground established for Confederate veterans and their families in Driftwood in 1896. Annual reunions for the veterans and their descendants have taken place there ever since.

Confederate veterans organized camps throughout the South in the late 1800s. Driftwood's Camp Ben McCulloch—named after Confederate brigadier general Ben McCulloch of Texas—was camp No. 946. Camp membership and attendance grew quickly following the first gathering in 1896, held on property donated by local veteran Joe Rogers. These photographs of reunion attendees were taken in 1915. (Both, G.B. Mading.)

This is another photograph from the Camp Ben McCulloch reunion in Driftwood. Camp Ben "grew to be the largest Confederate camp in existence," according to *100 Years on the Old Camp Ground*, by Lisa Shelton Robertson. (G.B. Mading)

This photograph was taken at a Mountain Remnant Brigade reunion in San Marcos in the 1890s. According to Charlie Haydon, lifelong Dripping Springs resident and owner of the historic Marshall-Chapman Bed and Breakfast, Dripping Spring's founding father Dr. Joseph Pound was a member of the Mountain Remnant Brigade. (Charlie Haydon.)

The presence and influence of the United Confederate Veterans was evident throughout the vicinity around Camp Ben. The area along Highway 290 through Oak Hill, south on Ranch Road 1826 past Camp Ben, through Driftwood out to Kyle, and back up to Austin through Buda was referred to as the Confederate Loop. The loop consisted of two roads: Ranch Road 1826, which was called the Confederate Highway as it veered south from Oak Hill before linking up in Kyle with the second road, the Jefferson Davis Highway, which headed north through Buda and back into Austin. (Charlie Haydon.)

The Driftwood Cemetery lies up the road from Camp Ben McCulloch. At least eight Civil War veterans are buried at this Texas historic site next to the Driftwood United Methodist Church.

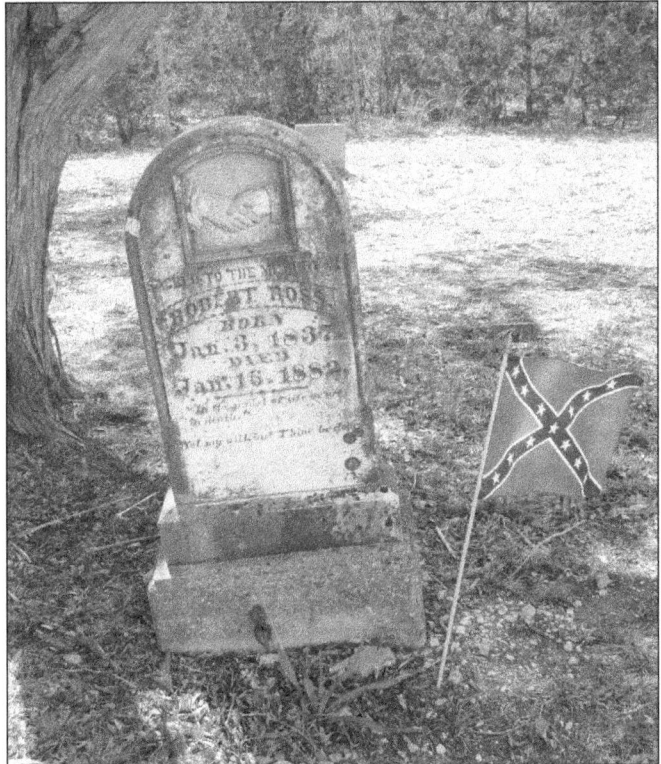

The Confederate flag represents a history that is acknowledged throughout cemeteries across the area, flown solely to honor the local men who fought in the Civil War. This Confederate flag waves over a grave in Pursley Cemetery, in the Mount Gainor area of Dripping Springs.

J.C. Breed is one of 16 Civil War veterans buried in Phillips Cemetery. Breed's name is also carved into one of the stone tabletops on the Camp Ben McCulloch reunion grounds.

Dripping Springs resident Jacob Quick's Confederate army muster roll shows he was "present" in 1863. This paperwork became important to veterans and widows applying for pensions in the Reconstruction years following the Civil War. (Travis Garnett.)

Jacob C. Quick and his wife, Mary Washington Quick, flourished in Dripping Springs after the Civil War. But the youngest of their 11 children, the beautiful Elizabeth "Lizzie" Quick—pictured here with her parents—came to a tragic end at age 20, probably not long after this photograph was taken. It seems the young woman from "the sticks" was lured to the "big city" of Austin by a reportedly handsome "traveling salesman." When the naive young Lizzie followed the man of her dreams to Austin, he forced her into a nightmare life of prostitution. The story goes that Lizzie's father repeatedly went to Austin to bring her home, but each time, the enterprising young pimp would come back to get her. It is likely Lizzie—with good reason—grew to fear this man who had so terribly deceived her. One story tells that upon hearing Lizzie's father was once again coming to retrieve his daughter, the young man shot and killed Lizzie, for which he was reportedly convicted and hanged. The other version of an unhappy ending is that young Lizzie died an early death from disease. Either way, the story tells of a tragedy that may seem surprising to some when considered in the context of the late 1800s, and it serves to remind parents and children today to be mindful of strangers. (Travis Garnett.)

This 1900 photograph of South Congress Avenue—now known as "SoCo"—shows that Austin roads were far from finished for wagons or cars. By wagon, the 25-mile trip would have taken the better part of a day, requiring an overnight stay before returning. The contrast between the family-oriented, churchgoing, agrarian atmosphere of Dripping Springs, and the fast-paced, "loose" lifestyle of the big city must have been startling for local residents who traveled to Austin for business or pleasure. (Vida Rippy family.)

The San Marcos Free Press reported in 1885 that a seven-and-a-half-foot, stuffed rattlesnake on display in the Chapman & Davis General Merchandise Store had been killed west of town. The rattlesnakes pictured here were shot in the Mount Gainor area around 1900. Rattlesnakes still abound in Central Texas, as do scorpions, fire ants, coyotes, poisonous centipedes, and feral hogs—all potentially harmful and sometimes fatal to humans. When one considers how common a Texan's exposure can be to blistering sun and dangerous predators, it is easy to see how the cowboy outfit of wide-brimmed hat, holstered guns, and thick leather boots is more common sense than fashion statement. (Travis Garnett.)

Cowboys are more than just a legend in Texas; theirs was a way of life for many locals and still is for some. Pictured are Alford Hill (left) and Walter Robinson. Alford was born in Hays County in 1893 and died in 1935. Members of the Hill family are still known as cowboys throughout the area. (Vida Rippy family.)

BEN W. TAYLOR, BORN APRIL 18, 1823
MARY DOLLAHITE TAYLOR, BORN 1851
BENNIE, AGE 11 YEARS
THOMAS, AGE 6 YEARS
BABY GIRL
DROWNED, FORKS ONION CREEKS SEPT. 6, 1882

Tragedy claimed the lives of the Taylor family on the night of September 6, 1882. Their home was situated between two forks of Onion Creek. During a torrential rain, the story is told that the father, Ben, rolled over in bed and was startled awake when his arm landed in water. Ben leaped out of bed, realizing the creeks were rising and flooding his home. He hollered to his wife, Mary, to grab their infant daughter and youngest son, while he made sure Bennie and the two eldest boys made it to safety. But it was too late. The flash flood roared through the forks and washed away the house and occupants. The two eldest boys, however, managed to grab onto treetops and perched in the branches all night as the floodwaters raged below. The next day, the Taylors' neighbor Jacob Frank Roberts spotted the two boys in the trees from a nearby hilltop. The boys were rescued and lived to tell the tragic tale. The five family members whose names are inscribed on this headstone in Phillips Cemetery were buried together in a common grave.

The area's first significant population surge took place after the Civil War. Despite the many hardships, tragedies, harsh weather, natural predators, and perils of the pioneer farm life, romance blossomed as more settlers arrived and flourished enough to feed families. Lonnie Griffin and Bethie Houchin, of Henly, are pictured while out for a buggy ride. It was undoubtedly a bumpy one considering there does not seem to be a road to follow. (Henly Homecoming.)

"First comes love, and then comes marriage." This elegant wedding dress is fairly unusual for 1901, especially for a bride in a mostly rural area. The bride's name is Betty Wegner, of Blanco, and she is marrying Willie Albert Breed, of Dripping Springs. The couple wed in Blanco before making their permanent home on the west side of Dripping Springs, toward Henly. Betty and Willie contributed five new residents to the area. Truman "Sonny" Breed Jr., one of their grandsons, was the founder of Breed & Co. Hardware, still in operation in Austin. (Carolyn Breed Gully.)

"Then comes baby"—maybe not in a baby carriage, but rocking in the arms of Grandma is better on the dry, hard ground of the farmer's fields. Having extended family nearby was the norm and a necessity while young parents plowed, planted, and harvested crops to feed the entire family. Pictured is "Sonny Boy" Mading as an infant in the arms of his grandmother Molly Elizabeth. (G.B. Mading.)

Building fences was one of the top priorities for landowners, as much for delineating property lines as for keeping valuable livestock from wandering. Settlers, farmers, and ranchers around Dripping Springs were, by modern standards, green and local when it came to securing materials to get the job done. They took advantage of the abundance of rocks throughout the area. This fence with a unique and decorative entrance pillar was reportedly built by slaves brought to the area with one of the settling families from the Deep South. To the credit of all who stacked rocks without mortar for fences like this, most still stand in silent tribute to the care and craft used to build them.

As the area developed, so did civil oversight. Boundaries for a new town called Liberty Hill were drawn up and approved by the Hays County Court of Commissioners and a county judge in 1891. But it was soon learned that a town named Liberty Hill already existed in nearby Williamson County. While meeting to discuss a new name, it is reported that one of the town leaders looked out a window and spotted a pile of driftwood near the proposed site of the post office, which was also to be built using driftwood. Driftwood was plentiful in the area because of frequent flooding of Onion Creek. The name *Driftwood* was promptly suggested for the town. Near the banks of Onion Creek, this modern-day pile of driftwood is heaped in the town of that name.

The town of Driftwood continued to grow and flourish, attracting families, pictured here in 1890, who created a community together, . By then, Driftwood had a post office, a school, two churches, a cotton gin, and a general store. A second store, a barbershop, and a blacksmith shop soon followed. (Pam Roberts McAfee.)

By 1898, the school in Driftwood was thriving. Classes met in the community church building, a common practice at the time. The two teachers pictured are Nannie Dorroh (left) and Mary Garrison. (Hays County Historical Commission.)

It appears there were many children attending school in Henly around this time, but with only one schoolteacher pictured to oversee them all. The enigmatic look on her face suggests she could handle the job. The boys kneeling in the dirt may have been required to hide their bare feet, which would have been considered an embarrassment for a formal photograph. The discomfort of kneeling on the hard ground helps explain the look on the boys' faces, especially in light of how long the shutter of a camera had to stay open to properly capture the image. This process also explains the distortion on the faces of some of the boys, who probably could not keep still quite that long. (Hays County Historical Commission.)

In this Henly school photograph, barefoot offenders kneeling in the dirt include girls. One young boy on the far left seems to gleefully defy the photographic barefoot ban, thrusting out his bare foot with hands on hips and a smirk on his face. The district number at the top of the picture is the number assigned to the Henly School charter. (Henly Homecoming.)

Another small but developing area around Dripping Springs was called Mount Sharp. This 1900 photograph includes family members joining students for a school picnic outing. (K. Cannon and Berkley families.)

The four Jennings brothers—Alex, Billy, Tom, and Jim—attended Mount Sharp School. Their father, L.S. Jennings, was born in the early 1800s in Connecticut. Jennings followed his carpentry trade to Richmond, Texas, where he took an 18-year-old bride, Hannah Elizabeth Staples. They had four sons who survived to adulthood, but Hannah did not survive her own adulthood. She died in 1855, at the age of 27. A few years later, L.S. brought his sons and a large flock of sheep to the Dripping Springs area, where he became one of the first settlers in Mount Sharp. Jim and Tom, two of the Jennings boys, are buried in the Mount Sharp cemetery. (K. Cannon and Berkley families.)

Mount Gainor, located about six miles southwest of Dripping Springs, was one of the more prosperous outlying villages. Spelled as often with *-er* as with an *-or*, Mount Gainor quickly grew to boast a store, a gristmill, and a sugarcane press for making sorghum molasses, as well as a church, school, and post office. This group of churchgoers attends services at the Mount Gainor schoolhouse. The women are dressed fashionably to include spats, which were considered a sign of prosperity. (K. Cannon and Berkley families.)

The town of Dripping Springs continued to grow at a pace generally a step or two ahead of its neighbors in education and culture. This 1899 photograph shows a group of graduating music students. The banner—dated June 22, 1899—indicates the students attend the Norwood Flowers Music School in Dripping Springs. (K. Cannon and Berkley families.)

As the rural communities around Dripping Springs grew, they were organized into common school districts to function locally while state education laws were established and developed. The common school districts were organized under common school trustees, a county superintendent, and county school trustees. As many as 16 local rural districts were formed around schools at Driftwood, Henly, Dripping Springs, Mount Gainor, Mount Sharp, Bell Springs, Darden Hill, Salem, Millseat, Fitzhugh Union, Haynie Flat, Bee Cave, Johnson, Hamilton Pool, Glenn, and Teck (located on property owned by T. Eck in what is now Lohman's Crossing in Lakeway). Judging from this 1870s School Director's Oath of Office form, the main requirement for a school director seemed to be not ever having participated in a duel. However, changes were coming that would establish a system of independent school districts with funding through taxation and much greater state oversight. (Hays County Historical Commission.)

Proceedings of School Directors.

List of Scholars Community No. 5 Dripping [Springs]

	Name	Age
1	Adams Evelina	13
2	" Sallie	12
3	" Warren	9
4	Bonds J.W. (Davis Co.)	12
5	" L. "	10
6	" S "	8
	Corn "	9
4	Durrenberger "	11
5	Fairchilds "	9
	Hunter Davis Co.	
6	Brackenridge Mc O.	11
7	" J.A.	8
8	Jolley	10
9	Kirk Mc E	9
10	Keese Mary	11
11	" Minnie	8
12	" Gideon	13
13	Schall John	12
14	" Phillip	9
15	Woods Willis	9
16	Wagner James	10
17	" Samuel	8

Register of School Officers and Term of Office.

School Community No. 10 Dripping Spring

NAMES OF OFFICERS	OFFICE	DATE OF COMMISSION			OFFICE EXPIRES		
		Month	Day	Year	Month	Day	Year
J.L. Wallace	President						
A.L. Davis	Trustees						
W.T. Chapman							

Organized December 12th 1876.

Apportionment Dec. 13, 1876. $40.60
29 Scholars 27.55
Total 68.15

In 1876, the State of Texas ratified a new constitution that set up a free public school system, but without teeth or funding, so the money had to come from county school funds. Fortunately, the state was out of debt and had previously transferred excess tax monies back to county coffers. Dripping Springs landowner and real estate speculator W.T. Chapman moved quickly in light of the 1876 state constitutional provisions and—along with founding father John Wallace and local merchant A.L. Davis—chartered a school in December 1876. With these prominent residents as trustees, and 29 scholars enrolled from the Dripping Springs Community School No. 5, along with the payment of a $68.15 fee, the Hays County School District No. 10 at Dripping Springs was established. (Hays County Historical Commission.)

Educator and traveling evangelist W.M. Jordan became convinced that Dripping Springs would be a perfect spot for a private boarding school following his arrival in the 1880s. A local community school called Walnut Springs Academy was in operation but, generally, those who could afford it sent their children to boarding schools. Jordan won the enthusiastic support of town leaders to build a local boarding school. Businessman W.T. Chapman donated land for the "Academy Block." A three-room stone building was estimated to cost $4,000. Dr. Joseph Pound offered care to patients in exchange for their skills on the project. In 1882, the school opened with an enrollment of 64 students. Dripping Springs Academy soon overshadowed Walnut Springs Academy, which closed around 1883. (Charlie Haydon.)

As the area grew and families flourished, there was no lack of students or teachers. Most of the area's longest-established families have provided multiple generations of teachers for local students. Pictured is Dr. Pound's daughter, Georgia Pound Cavett, with her students in 1915. Miss Georgia was a teacher in Dripping Springs schools for more than 20 years and is credited with organizing the first parent-teacher group. She passed away in 1968, just short of her 100th birthday. (Hays County Historical Commission.)

Pictured at right is Dr. Pound's granddaughter Marguerite—daughter of Georgia Pound Cavett—sitting with a teacher during the 1910–1911 school year in her grandparents' backyard at what is now the Dr. Pound Farmstead Museum in Dripping Springs, more commonly referred to locally as the "Pound House." (K. Cannon and Berkley families.)

Another community school was established south of Henly in the 1870s. Distinguishing this school from the other common schools throughout the Dripping Springs area was the fact that the Peyton Colony School was built to educate the children of freed slaves following the Civil War. The Peyton Colony settlement was established around 1865 by a former slave named Peyton Roberts, who was born in Virginia and emancipated in Lockhart, Texas. Peyton Colony had its own post office from 1898 to 1909. A second post office operated from 1918 to 1930 under the name of Board House, because the post office was located in the community's first boardinghouse, run by A.V. Walker. Peyton Colony still exists today, although the number of descendants currently living there is down to just a handful.

The Peyton Colony School was isolated from the surrounding communities by culture and color barriers throughout its history of operation from 1877 to 1963. Students living in the freedmen's colony attended the small, wooden schoolhouse from first through eighth grades. After eighth grade, students could continue their educations in Austin or in the nearby town of Blanco. Following World War II, however, most of the colony's "young folks" wanted the city life and sold their family properties to move to Austin and beyond. By the year 2000 (the latest census figures available), Peyton Colony's population had dwindled to 30.

The heart of Peyton Colony was and still is Mount Horeb Baptist Church. The church was established in 1874 by a freedman named Jack Burch, who arrived at the colony from Tennessee and pitched a tent for the first meeting. Land for a church building was donated by Peyton Colony resident Jim Upshaw. Initially, church meetings were held in the wooden one-room schoolhouse. Nearly 150 years later, Sunday morning services continue to be held in the peaceful, pretty country church and are open to the public.

Coffee, City, Jones, and Jackson are among the Petyon Colony family names honored with memorial ribbons inside the Mount Horeb Baptist Church sanctuary. The congregation is down to fewer than a dozen who faithfully attend. The pastor who serves them travels some 50 miles weekly each way. But a warmer welcome could not be had by any stranger who visits a Sunday-morning service. Once a year, the church also hosts a Juneteenth event for all of the surrounding communities to join them in celebrating the anniversary of Emancipation.

Peyton Roberts was born into slavery in Virginia, in 1820, on the plantation of William Roberts. After gaining his freedom along with several other formerly enslaved families at the end of the Civil War, Peyton led them by wagon to the Texas Hill Country. They built cabins on public land, which became theirs through preemption, and became known as Peyton Colony, or Peyton's Colony. Like their neighbors throughout the Dripping Springs area, the freedmen and their families farmed and raised livestock. The enterprising Peyton, along with others in the community, also built a limekiln to make mortar for buildings in neighboring towns. Peyton died in 1888. His grave is among those of 176 former residents of his freedmen's colony.

Martha Steward was a former slave to the McQueen family. This photograph of Martha was taken at a portrait studio in Mobile, Alabama. The McQueens came to Central Texas from Alabama. Following Emancipation, Martha and her son Robert stayed on with the McQueen family for quite some time before moving on. Descendants of the McQueens in the area have not succeeded in learning what happened to Martha and Robert, although it is suspected they may have made their way to another freedmen's colony in the Blanco area. (G.B. Mading.)

Tom Quick's store was located in the Mount Gainor area. Notations on the photograph indicate this picture was taken around 1900 and that a small porch, a gas pump, and kerosene containers were later added when the Model T car came in. Pictured standing nearby are Tom Quick and two of his children. One story about the lack of windows is that it helped prevent robberies after hours, because thieves could not see the contents inside. Another unsubstantiated story, which may or may not have had to do with the lack of windows, is that the location may have been used to buy and sell slaves. (Travis Garnett.)

It is a good thing Tom Quick had a prosperous store at Mount Gainor to feed his large family. Tom and his wife, Alice Calhoun Quick, are pictured here about 1915, surrounded by 10 of their 12 children "borned from 1892–1913." Other notations on this photograph indicate that "Little Jakob" was their first child but had "already died," and that "Vonna had already married and gone." (Travis Garnett.)

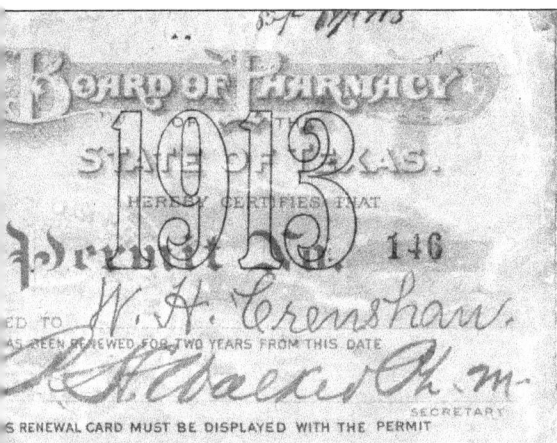

By the late 1800s, the town of Dripping Springs was described as "crowded" in the *San Marcos Free Press*. In 1894, the paper reported, "Dripping Springs [is] well supplied with doctors—Pound, Steel, Russell, and Shelton. Also a dentist, Stewart." The report went on to say, "School opens first of October. Families are moving into town." By this time, Dripping Springs boasted several amenities including stores, churches, schools, and blacksmiths. In 1900, druggist George McCuistion opened his pharmacy, then sold it to William Hill "W.H." Crenshaw five years later. Crenshaw's permit from the Board of Pharmacy in the State of Texas, issued in 1915, shows he is licensed "for towns less than 1,000 inhabitants." (G.B. Mading.)

The Crenshaw pharmacy stood on the south side of Mercer Street in Dripping Springs. On the left side of the store, in the background, the town blacksmith shop can be seen. Pictured here in front of the pharmacy are, from left to right, Anna Crenshaw, Dora P. Crenshaw, W.H. Crenshaw, Dr. Berkley, Dave Wesley Crenshaw, Webb Hudson, and Caudential Waite. The building still stands on Mercer Street, but not in its original spot. It was moved several times before it landed in its final location in 1972, adjacent to the old Dripping Springs Academy building, which later became the Rambo Masonic Lodge. The exterior of the old drugstore was plastered and now sits covered in vines with a rusty tin roof. (G.B. Mading.)

The A.L. Davis Mercantile Store, pictured here in 1891, sat prominently on Mercer Street, the main dirt road through Dripping Springs. The general merchandise store was located on the first floor. The second floor was used for meetings by various organizations. A rainwater barrel was installed on the west side. It is reported that Davis ran a water line to his house two blocks away from the store's rainwater collection system and that the water rights remained in place when he later sold his house. The Haydon Cotton Gin is visible in the background on the left. The gin was built in the 1890s and changed hands several times before Charles Haydon bought it in 1924. This is the only photograph that has surfaced of the Dripping Springs gin, which burned to the ground in 1940. (G.B. Mading.)

Residents throughout the neighboring communities and villages pitched in to help each other, so it was not unusual to see men, boys, and animals from more than one family working together to help cultivate a neighbor's property. Shown here are members of the Quick and Seals families, neighbors in the Mount Gainor area. There was also a lot of shared labor freely exchanged with the freedmen farmers of Peyton Colony. Descendants on both sides of the color line have spoken fondly of their families helping each other with fields and livestock, celebrating each other's holidays, and bearing each other's burdens in times of struggle and grief. (Travis Garnett.)

Despite the hard work needed to carve out a living, there is plenty of evidence of an avid recreational life throughout the area. This 1900 Driftwood baseball team pictured clearly took the game seriously. Their competitors included a similarly outfitted team from Dripping Springs with "DS" emblazoned on their uniform shirts. (Hall family.)

The village of Henly had grown enough by the early 1900s to boast its own post office. This photograph of Overton H. Oldham's store and post office was taken in 1914. Residents are bundled up against what appears to be a freeze, evidenced by a thick row of icicles along the storefront overhang. O.H. Oldham sold the store in 1922 to John Ross—previously the postmaster of Mount Sharp—who then became the postmaster at Henly. (Henly Homecoming.)

Three

PROGRESS

Family, faith, farming, education, commerce, and community were all a part of everyday life around Dripping Springs in the 1920s and 1930s—and so was fun. In good times or bad, people young and old seemed to share a playfulness, expressed in community games and pastimes like basketball, baseball, swimming, fishing, and hunting. One favorite local game was dominoes, particularly a game called 42, which is still played in the area. Pictured here is the Langston family in 1931, enjoying an outdoor session of 42. (G.B. Mading.)

The fish were obviously biting the day this photograph was taken. Fishing was another popular pastime for men and women alike. The hats worn by these friends depict a variety of eras, from a prairie bonnet to what appears to be a 1930s fedora, popularly worn by notorious gangsters of the era—and apparently by men who went fishing in rural areas. (Lila Thielepape Gillespie.)

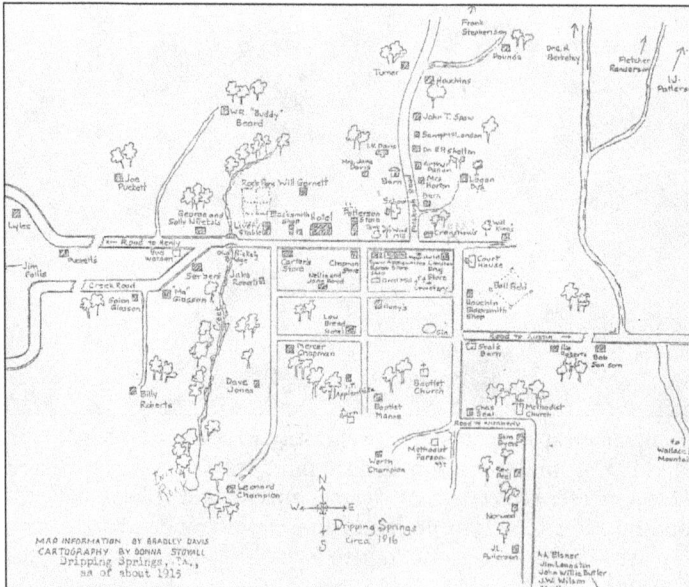

By 1916, according to Bradley Davis's recollections drawn here, Dripping Springs had a gristmill, cotton gin, several stores, two hotels, two blacksmith shops, a drugstore, a barbershop, a baseball field, two churches, a school, and a courthouse. Now, the "Road to Austin" is Highway 290; the "Road to Henly" is Mercer Street. Creek Road no longer links to Mercer due to a longer 290. The Pound homestead is now preserved at Founder's Park. (Travis Garnett.)

Rosa Lyle gives Will Spaw a helping hand as he scrambles up out of a limekiln in 1919. Lime was quarried all over Central Texas. The local kiln was used to make mortar for the construction of the Dripping Springs Academy building. Limekilns were commonly used to produce mortar for buildings because cement was not available for construction. The turnaround time to produce a typical load of lime mortar in the kiln was about a week; the kiln took a day to load, three days to fire, two days to cool, and one more day to unload. (Travis Garnett.)

A young man looks on as this picture is taken of an early-1900s Dripping Springs girls' basketball team. Athletic teams were an integral part of education around Dripping Springs from the beginning, for both boys and girls, and have continued to be a high priority in local schools. (Travis Garnett.)

Early 1900's Dripping Springs Girls Basket Ball team

Young women were employed as teachers at an early age. The notations on this school photograph from the early 1900s show the teacher is Vonna Quick, on the far left, looking not much older than her students. Of her students, nine were apparently relatives, perhaps helping Quick keep her classroom under control. (K. Cannon and Berkley families.)

Lou Breed stands in front of her boardinghouse in the 1920s. On April 6, 1923, the San Marcos Record reported: "Madames Glosson and Breed bought the Perry place and opened a hotel, where the traveling public can find first class accommodations." The building still stands at the corner of College Street and Highway 290. At the time of the photograph, the boardinghouse faced the Haydon Cotton Gin, which later burned down. (Carolyn Breed Gully.)

Progress began to find its way to the area in the early 1900s. This fascinating picture from 1910 shows industrious Henly resident Tom Jennings using a six-mule team and special wagon to haul a massive boiler made of iron more than 25 miles from Austin to Henly. Considering the weight of the boiler and the condition of the roads over that distance, the feat was an ambitious undertaking and required ingenuity along the way. Word traveled fast, and people came out all along the hilly route to watch. Jennings succeeded, and the boiler was installed at the Beauchamp mill and gin in place of the old one, which had "burnt out." The boiler helped Henly farmers continue turning their cotton and grains into cash and food for their families. (Henly Homecoming.)

A steam tractor probably sounded like a great idea to farmers who had to provide their own "steam" while tied to a team of mules or horses to plow the hard, rocky ground in the early 1900s. But these farmers quickly found out as evidenced in the second image that a steam tractor may have been more trouble than it was worth when it had to be hooked up to a team of horses and pulled out of the mud. (Travis Garnett.)

The availability of field contraptions increased as new ideas about how to use machinery to ease the arduous tasks of farming came and went. But farmers learned to keep some extra "old-fashioned" help standing by in case things did not go as planned. That seems to be the case in the scene pictured, involving what appears to be an engine-operated stump puller. (Travis Garnett.)

The women's work was also never done (as the idiom goes). The chore of drawing water by the bucketful from a well certainly needed modernization. Indoor plumbing did not become commonplace in the area until the 1940s, so women still faced about 20 more years of water hauling in 1922, when this picture was taken. No doubt, water conservation was a normal way of life for local residents, simply because of the sheer labor involved to access it. (Lila Thielepape Gillespie.)

Many boys and girls around Dripping Springs still learn to safely shoot guns at a young age. Guns and hunting were an important part of a natural way of life throughout the area's history, sometimes for sport, but mostly to help provide food and protection from wild animals. Pictured here with his rifle in the early 1940s, Dripping Springs resident John Gillespie is about 14 years old. (Lila Thielepape Gillespie.)

Laurel Hall, of Driftwood, is said to have killed the area's last mountain lion. Hall is pictured here, showing off the cat in front of the Driftwood Store in 1919. The mountain lion was killed during a foxhunt, which had become a popular pastime around the area. (Hall family.)

The length of the tail is one of the main differences between a large mountain lion and the much smaller bobcat. This wildcat with the bobbed tail was killed by area residents Bruce B. Mading (left) and Forrest Hauseman (holding the trophy) in 1923. Perhaps the hunt was also a training exercise to teach the tiny puppy perched in the car some new tricks. (G.B. Mading.)

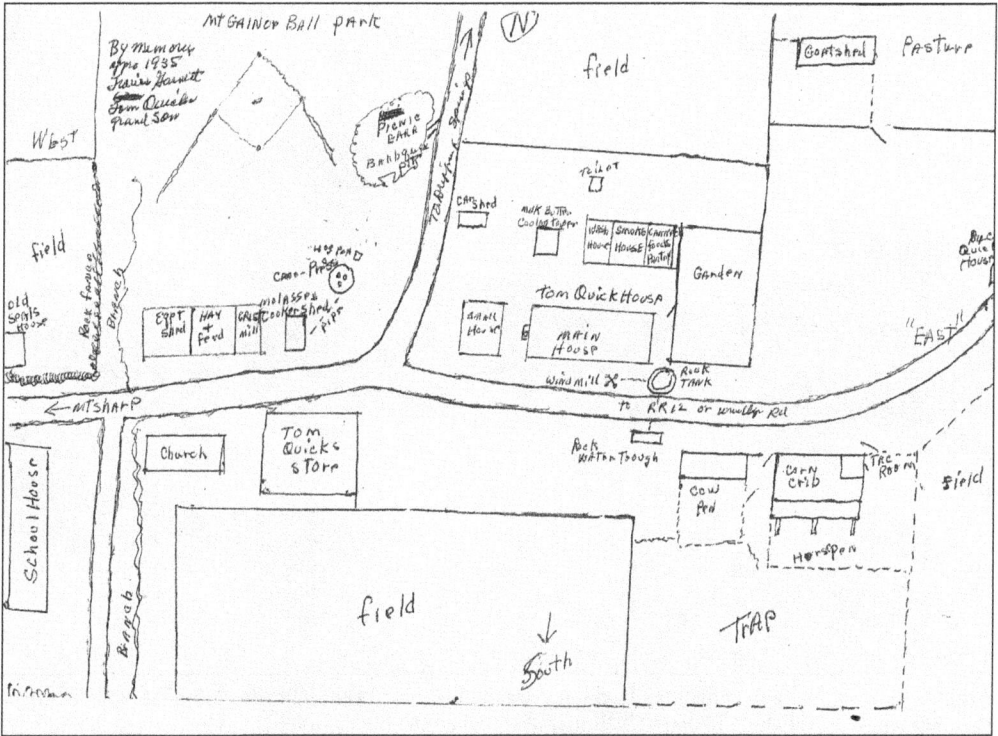

By the 1930s, the Mount Gainor area of Dripping Springs had its own school, store, church, baseball field, gristmill, and sorghum molasses mill. With a creek running through it, a growing population, and good roads to get everywhere as cars became more commonplace, Mount Gainor was a thriving and popular place to live. This map was drawn from memory by Tom Quick's grandson Travis Garnett. Travis also had an uncle in the area named Percy Garnett. Travis told the story of how his uncle came to kill one of his own Calhoun in-laws, not too far from the Y-shaped intersection shown here. (Travis Garnett.)

Percy Garnett, seated in the middle of this family photograph with his hat on his lap, was one of the sons of William Garnett, a prominent resident around the Dripping Springs area. Percy is pictured with his wife on the left. The couple had six boys but no girls. Percy's wife was a Calhoun. She may have been able to endure the hardships of a rural farming life, but she was likely unprepared for the tragedy that befell her young family through her husband's murderous actions in the 1930s. (Travis Garnett.)

The Calhouns and the Garnetts lived at Mount Sharp, about 10 miles from Mount Gainor. Percy Garnett ambushed Robert Calhoun along the Mount Gainor Road connecting the two communities and shot him to death. Apparently, there was an ongoing feud between the two men over mules breaking into each other's pastures and eating the feed. Garnett's final solution involved lying in wait alongside the Mount Gainor Road for Robert Calhoun's wagon. Calhoun was hauling a load of sugarcane to the Mount Gainor molasses mill when Garnett ambushed him and, according to local lore, shot Calhoun in the back. Ironically, the team of mules pulling the wagon allegedly broke loose and showed up in someone else's field. There was also a young boy in the wagon with Calhoun at the time of the murder, but it is not clear who the boy was or what his relationship was to Calhoun. The boy was not physically injured and allegedly jumped out of the wagon, hid in the bushes, and then ran to a nearby home to report what had happened. Although tried and convicted, Garnett was not executed by either Hays County or the State of Texas. Before 1923, counties across Texas executed their own by hanging. After 1923, all executions were carried out by the state at Huntsville, in the electric chair. But Percy Garnet was pardoned by Gov. Miriam "Ma" Ferguson—the first female governor of Texas—and served just 10 years in the state penitentiary for the murder.

It has been said that every flat piece of land around Dripping Springs was used to grow or attempt to grow cotton at one time or another. The majority of the founders and farmers drawn to the area came from Southern states where cotton was king. They brought their love of the fluffy white "vegetable fiber" with them, along with their knowledge of planting, growing, and harvesting cotton as a cash crop and a means to provide clothing. Although cotton did not prove to be a permanent fixture in the local economy, it helped area farmers get through the mid-1920s drought and the country's later slide into economic depression. Pictured are Tula Quick (left) and Hattie Garnett, whose families farmed cotton around Mount Gainor until about 1940. (Travis Garnett.)

According to one report about the cotton industry in Hays County, "Gins were built in all areas . . . where there was land suitable for farming." Henly had a gin, as did Driftwood. The Driftwood gin (pictured) was owned and operated by Charles Haydon, before he moved to Dripping Springs and bought the last gin to operate there. By the time the Haydon gin burned to the ground in Dripping Springs in 1940, cotton farming had greatly declined across the area. (Charlie Haydon.)

This gold ring is made from a gold piece earned by a Dripping Springs family in 1914 from the sale of cotton bales, which were valued at about $2.50 each. The family would take their cotton to the gin to be shipped out, but they would also keep enough to card and make quilts and other household items for themselves. The gold ring is a valuable reminder of the important contribution cotton made to sustaining the people and growth of the area.

Young Lila Thielepape is pictured with her mother and brother in the 1930s, walking down the west side of Congress Avenue in Austin. Like many of the people living around rural Dripping Springs, the Thielepapes were educated and well dressed. Lila's family made regular trips to Austin to sell produce and butter to supplement their income, but their rural life in Dripping Springs was far from the city lights. The family finally got electricity at their place in 1939, thanks to a local politician, from nearby Johnson City, named Lyndon B. Johnson. Before that time, Lila recalls her dad going into Dripping Springs to buy 100 pounds of ice, which he would put in an icehouse where the cream was stored. Once a week, Lila and her family would churn the cream to butter, wrap it, and take it in to Austin to sell door-to-door or to grocers. (Lila Thielepape Gillespie.)

People around Dripping Springs took advantage of their proximity to the city of Austin as transportation improved. Thomas Gillespie, Lila Thielepape Gillespie's father-in-law, worked in the downtown American Express office in the 1920s and 1930s. The office was located at the train station on Congress Avenue and primarily served as a shipping and freight office. The busy office would have been a great place to bring back news to Dripping Springs from around the country and the world. (Lila Thielepape Gillespie.)

It is hard to say which is more surprising about this letter sent from the State of Texas Comptroller's Department in 1926—the image of a Confederate flag on state letterhead or the warmth and personal regard expressed by a government official to the recipient. Especially entertaining is the second paragraph, in which comptroller Sam Houston Terrell states, "My ambition is to continue to serve you faithfully and to increase your pension payments with each semi-annual apportionment." How shocking it would be to receive a letter like this from a state official today! Less shocking, the letter also references "the present overdrawn condition of the Confederate Pension Fund, recently referred to in newspaper reports." (G.B. Mading.)

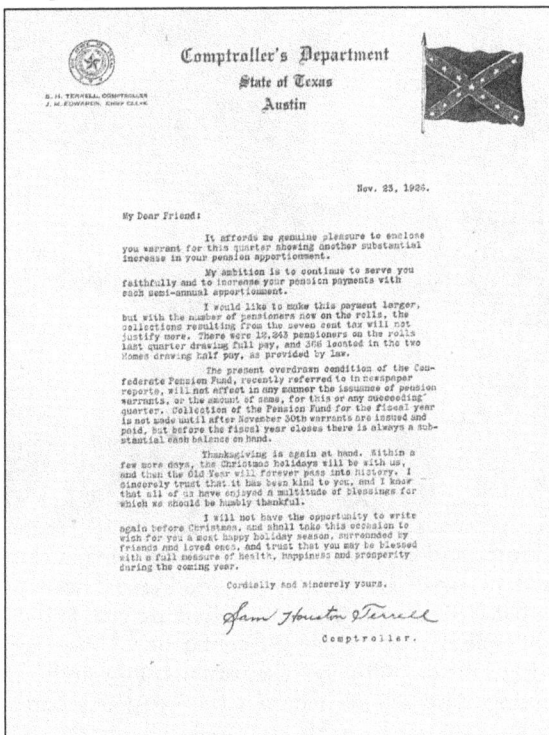

Despite progress and modern ideas, local color lines were still clearly drawn in the 1930s. This photograph shows young John Gillespie, of Austin, being cared for by a black nanny in the early 1930s. John's family later moved to Dripping Springs, where he met and married Lila Thielepape. Lila, born and raised in Dripping Springs, thought John was "sophisticated" because he was familiar with being around people of different skin colors. Despite being brought up in a small town deep in the heart of Texas, Lila does not personally recall any episodes of racial tension or local violence during her upbringing. (Lila Thielepape Gillespie.)

Transportation options were rapidly changing by the 1920s with the introduction of automobiles and the expansion of railroads. Children did not seem to lack their own forms of transportation either. Posing with this nimble-looking goat and cart for a souvenir photograph, young John Gillespie appears capable and confident. Chances are John and the goat could have outpaced the cars of the day. Children used animals for transportation from the beginning around Dripping Springs. Most schoolchildren in the area doubled up or even tripled up on the bare backs of horses or mules to ride to and from school well into the 1930s and 1940s. (Lila Thielepape Gillespie.)

What a catch! Pictured are locals Irene Combs (left) and Frances Berkley, showing off their big catfish in 1937 while enjoying some outdoor recreation at a fishing camp on the Pedernales River, between Dripping Springs and Johnson City. (Carolyn Breed Gully.)

A popular pastime in the 1920s and 1930s was called "Kodakin'," what might be referred to today as a "Kodak moment." Young people of the time dressed up—despite rural, outdoor settings—for these photographic adventures. This group managed to find a gravel mound in a creek for this Kodakin' moment. (Vida Rippy family.)

Cotton farming started to decline in the 1920s. The soil was never ideal and had slowly been depleted or lost to erosion. Local farmers turned to corn and tomato crops, and Henly became well known for producing tomatoes. But the land never provided much beyond subsistence. That changed, however, as landowners began to realize new value in their property as breeding and feeding grounds for livestock—especially sheep and goats, whose wool and mohair quickly became the area's new "cash crop." This herd of Angora goats belonged to Dripping Springs resident Wolf Cobb, one of the earliest local ranchers to seize the opportunity. In 1924, Cobb drove more than 300 head of Angora goats from Kimble County to Hays County. Cobb successfully raised herds until his death in 1967. (Clarence Cobb.)

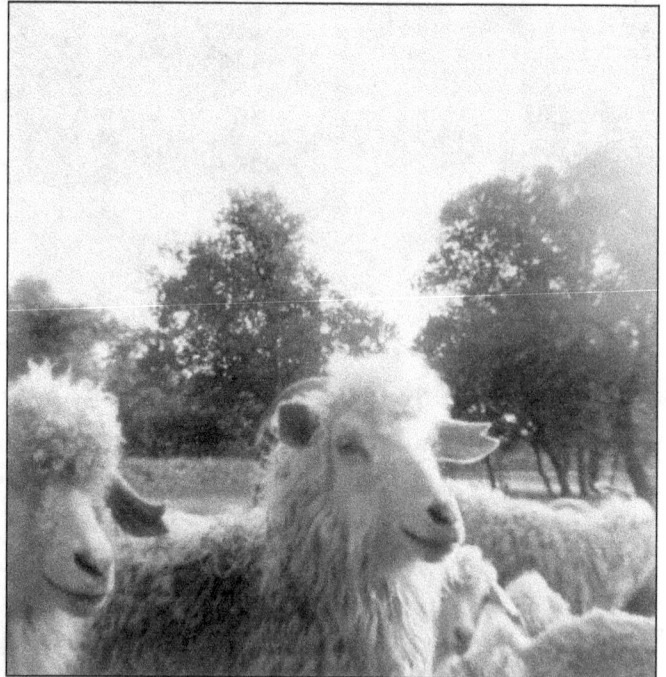

Ranchers applied distinctive earmarks to their goats, much like cattle brands. Both ears were uniformly marked with two separate shapes—one on the right ear and one on the left. The Cobb earmarks were a "swallow fork" on the left ear and a "crop and under slope" on the right ear. The rapid increase in the area goat population after Cobb brought his herd made earmarks critical for ranchers to identify their income-producing animals. (Clarence Cobb.)

Over in Driftwood, goats also thrived. According to Carl Wait's book *The Complete History of Dripping Springs and the P.A. Smith Survey*, a report in the *San Marcos Record* stated, "Between the years of 1925 to 1927, Angora goats had increased from 2,150 to 25,690 in Hays County." Pictured is rancher Syd Hall, examining part of his herd on his Elder Hill Road property. (Hall family.)

In 1937, Dripping Springs businessman Will Crow built a warehouse for the storage and sale of wool and mohair. It proved a busy and lucrative business for Crow and area ranchers. The US government also began paying a mohair subsidy. Will Crow later sold his business to the Rippy family, who opened Rippy Feed on Mercer Street. Before Crow got into the wool and mohair markets, he operated a general merchandise store; his name is advertised on the side of the building to the right of the Mobil gas station. (Travis Garnett.)

The Rambo Masonic Lodge No. 426 was chartered in 1875 and named after local landowner R.J. Rambo. Many of the most prominent men around Dripping Springs became influential members. Freemasonry claims to be the oldest and largest fraternal organization in the world. The Rambo Lodge in Dripping Springs occupied three different lodge halls prior to its present location. Since 1952, the lodge has been meeting on the second floor of the historic Dripping Springs Academy Building— fitting given the Masons' commitment to public education. This photograph of the upper meeting room was taken in 2011.

One wall of the second-floor Masonic Lodge meeting room in the old Dripping Springs Academy building is lined with framed photographs of area men who have served as worshipful masters. According to the lodge's centennial brochure from 1975, "Rambo Lodge was strengthened by the merging of Driftwood Lodge #1221 . . . in 1943. Since that time, many active members of Rambo Lodge have come from the Driftwood area." Several also joined from the Henly area. The Rambo Lodge is a "moon lodge," meaning the lodges' monthly meeting days are determined by the full moon and fall on the first Saturday on or following a full moon. This was likely originally practiced before electricity because of the light provided at night on a full moon, so Masons could see their way home.

The legendary Dr. E.P. (Edgar Poe) Shelton, of Dripping Springs, is second only in local lore and stature to Dr. Joseph Pound. Dr. Shelton, pictured here on the right in 1946, is said to have delivered nearly 4,000 babies—including his own 15 children—during his 55-year doctoring career throughout the area. Remarkably, only two women died in childbirth while under his care. Dr. Shelton reportedly came to Dripping Springs in the 1890s, as a young man recently graduated from medical college in Kentucky, to learn from Dr. Pound—who also studied medicine in Kentucky—before moving on. But Dr. Shelton fell in love with the town and with a local girl, married her, and stayed put for the rest of his career and life. He also served two terms in the state legislature in Austin. In his old account books, Dr. Shelton often referred to his patients with nicknames and sometimes a remark about a person's character. Some of the nicknames later recalled by his widow include "Cross-eyed Twiddle," "Dead-eye Jones," "Trigger-eye Smith," and "Buttermilk Bill," next to whose name Dr. Shelton wrote, "the laziest man on earth." Dr. Shelton, the son of a Confederate veteran, was also instrumental in organizing the Camp Ben McCulloch Confederate Veterans Reunion. Dr. Shelton died after a very brief illness in the spring of 1946, no doubt shortly after this photograph was taken. (Travis Garnett.)

The transition in transportation from horseback to horsepower was a slow and gradual process. Cars were convenient, but horses were a way of life. Roads in the area were not always car-worthy. Ranch Road 12 was not paved until 1947, and elevated bridges over the creeks were not common because of budget constraints. Communications with the outside world were evolving as well. By the 1930s, mail from Austin was delivered regularly throughout the area. According to Henly resident Shelton Jennings, whose Grandfather Ross was postmaster there, baby chicks were often delivered through the Post Office Department, forerunner of the US Postal Service. Telephone services came more quickly to the area, with reports in 1906 of plans to install a switchboard in Driftwood. And thanks to the combined efforts of local businessman Will Crow and his friend Lyndon B. Johnson—who became a prominent politician locally before becoming the 36th president of the United States—electricity and city water began flowing into the area by the late 1930s. (Vida Rippy family.)

Blacksmith shops remained useful for many years after the advent of automobiles. Locals still depended on horses for work and for getting around. Will S. Garnett set up a blacksmith shop along Mercer Street in Dripping Springs in the early 1900s. Like many blacksmiths, Garnett also provided funeral services and served as a funeral director. As cars and roads slowly improved, automobiles eventually dominated the local landscape. Blacksmith shops disappeared, and garages with automobile mechanics multiplied along Mercer Street. Highway 290 was built in 1937, although it was not completed until 1958. (Travis Garnett.)

Local ingenuity continued to adapt to modern technology and innovations. Following the rise of the automobile, the Garnett family transitioned from blacksmithing to automobile mechanics. Fathers and sons showed a knack for machinery. Travis Garnett's father, Bill, was a master mechanic. Bill constructed this waterpowered machine to charge car batteries at his garage, which he ran until his untimely death in 1948. In 2011, the Garnett family still owned and operated the 5-G Garage on Mercer Street in Dripping Springs. (Travis Garnett.)

Education was also improving throughout the area. In 1930, nineteen-year-old Oleta Dobbins of Austin was offered $100 a month to run the Fitzhugh Union School in Hays County. Oleta got more than she bargained for with 50 students in several grades. She made a deal with the school trustees to hire a man to co-teach with her and share her salary. The young man hired to teach the upper grades was Willie James "Sonny Boy" Mading. Once again, Oleta got more than she bargained for and soon agreed to become his wife. The happy couple later relocated to Austin. (Hays County Historical Commission.)

78

The Fitzhugh Union School was located in Hays County, near the Travis County line, in an area referred to as Fitzhugh but officially named Cedar Valley. The school was named called "Union" because students who lived in both Hays and Travis Counties attended. In an interview with local historian J. Marie Bassett, former Fitzhugh Union schoolteacher Oleta Mae Dobbins Mading—aged 90 when interviewed—fondly remembered her students. On one afternoon, Oleta reported with a smile, she kept taking away pocketknives from a mischievous student named Buster Meyers. By day's end, Oleta had collected 12 pocketknives, which she said Buster carried "just to aggravate [her]." (Hays County Historical Commission.)

The Dripping Springs School continued to grow, and athletics was always part of the curriculum. Pictured here is a girls' basketball team in the 1930s, complete with uniforms and coaches. They played outdoors on a dirt court. (Travis Garnett.)

The Dripping Springs boys' basketball team is pictured in 1930. The team played basketball on the athletic field near the Academy Block, where two wooden basketball goals were erected. Student athletes in Dripping Springs did not have a gymnasium until the early 1950s. (Travis Garnett.)

The Dripping Springs six-man football team used the athletic field by the Academy Block for games and practices. Seen in the background of this practice session photograph, on the left side, is one of the basketball practice goals. Also pictured behind the team are the school outhouses, one for girls and one for boys. This picture appeared in the 1948 *Tigerland* high school yearbook with two blank spaces where the outhouses are located. The outhouses were probably covered with sheets of paper, leaving entire chunks of the trees blanked out. The first indoor restrooms were not installed in Dripping Springs school facilities until 1949. (Travis Garnett.)

A second story was added to the Dripping Springs Academy building in 1922. Resident Clarence Cobb likes to tell how his classmate Grady Moore would climb out a second-story window and hang from the ledge so the teacher could not find him. When she left the classroom to look for him, Grady would climb back in and be seated when she returned. Grady later became the superintendent of Dripping Springs schools. The Academy building was the town's primary education facility until 1949 and was designated a Texas Historic Landmark in 1967.

The Allen Stephenson School building was built in 1939, and named after a 15-year old Dripping Springs student who died from complications following a baseball injury. Local labor built the school under the Works Progress Administration (WPA), the largest of the federal New Deal agencies designed to put Americans to work after the Great Depression. The Stephenson building served as a high school for 10 years. Subsequent uses have included community meetings, church services, auditorium functions, school administration offices, and Hays County offices.

At an elevation of just over 1,000 feet and named for the day of the week the first surveyors arrived, Friday Mountain lies between Driftwood and what was once known as Cedar Valley. A secondary school—among the first in Central Texas—operated here from 1852 to 1872. The property changed hands several times until it was purchased by Walter Prescott Webb, from the University of Texas at Austin. Webb restored and expanded the former school facilities and opened the Friday Mountain Boys Camp in 1947. Local residents have happy memories of summers at the camp, but many came from elsewhere. Pictured is camper Skippy Bohn. (Bradley Davis family.)

Bear Creek runs through the Friday Mountain property, so swimming was a popular camp pastime. Other activities included hiking, horseback riding, competitive games, and sports. The camp averaged about 120 boys per session. A girls' camp was equally well attended. The camps closed in the 1980s, and the property was purchased by a religious group from California. Their Hindu temple is a startling site that towers above the trees along Ranch Road 1826 between Driftwood and Oak Hill. (Bradley Davis family.)

Young people have long sought relief from the Texas heat by the cooling waters found across the area in numerous creeks and swimming holes. Pictured are Ruby Lee Davis (left) and Sally Jo Rust, from Henly. Girls and boys alike learned from an early age how to scramble barefoot up and down limestone banks to cool off. (Henly Homecoming.)

Little Carolyn Breed and her aunts and cousin enjoyed their childhood days playing together in the cool creeks on family ranches. A favorite pastime that put their outdoor time to good use was called caning or thrashing pecans. The adults would use long cane poles—also used for fishing—to thrash the branches of pecan trees in the early fall. The popular nuts would be gathered up by the children to take home for making treats. Sweets, like pralines and pecan pies, are still commonly sold and enjoyed throughout the Texas Hill Country. (Carolyn Breed Gully.)

Turkey farming became popular in the 1940s and 1950s as another way to produce income by selling the meat to local markets. Pictured here is Bessie Clifton Combs with her flock of turkeys on the Combs Ranch, located on Creek Road in Dripping Springs. (Carolyn Breed Gully.)

Local grocery stores, like the Glosson's Red & White Grocery in Dripping Springs, knew the meaning of "buy local." These independent, small-town grocers depended on local farmers and ranchers for produce, dairy, and meats, like turkey, beef, and chicken. Pictured to the far right of the grocery is an honor-system icehouse where perishables might also have been temporarily stored before refrigeration. Glosson operated a Red & White grocery in this location until the building burned down in 1951. (Travis Garnett.)

Churches grew with the population in the thriving Dripping Springs area. This 1942 photograph shows the new Church of Christ building on Mercer Street, which was constructed before Highway 290 was completed or Mercer Street was paved. The church originally faced east, but was turned to face north in the 1950s when the so-called superhighway came through and clipped some of the church's land. The congregation later moved to the Meadow Oaks subdivision area, and the old building became home to the Dripping Springs City Hall offices at 290 East and Mercer Street. (Grady Moore.)

The Methodist church in Driftwood was originally referenced in the historical record as far back as 1879. In continuous use since it was built in 1884, the church is now a registered Texas historic site. The Methodist congregation shared its sanctuary with the Driftwood Baptist congregation after the Baptist church building was destroyed by fire in 1911. Descendants of the pioneers who established Driftwood still attend Driftwood Methodist Church.

This 1944 photograph shows the Reverend J.N. Marshall standing in front of the Henly Baptist Church. The church continues to host the annual Henly Homecoming reunion for anyone who has ever called Henly home. The event is open to the public. (Henly Homecoming.)

The young folks of Henly were hardly hicks, as can be seen in this engaging photograph of Normaleen Jennings and Vahn Adams. The nation had finally recovered from the Great Depression, and even folks out in the country had access to fashionable clothes and cars, if not paved roads yet. (Henly Homecoming.)

By T. GARNETT

Times were good in Dripping Springs in 1940. Fritz Miller owned the Texaco station on Mercer Street and decided to build a small café next door as an investment. Pictured are Hattie (left) and Lois Garnett in front of the cute café, taken over by the Glossons and renamed Bonnie's Cafe, after their daughter. The Glossons gave up the café in 1956 and took their entrepreneurial skills down the street to run the Red & White Grocery. The Rock Cafe building was converted into a residence in 1965 before being put to use as office space in 1992. (Travis Garnett.)

There was plenty for the young people to do in the 1940s. This 1941 ticket to a University of Texas (UT) football game in Austin cost just 25¢ at the gate for fifth through eighth graders. According to the Dripping Springs *Tiger Cry* school publication, nearly three dozen local students went to the game. It was worth the trip when UT shut out Rice University 40-0. (Lila Thielepape Gillespie.)

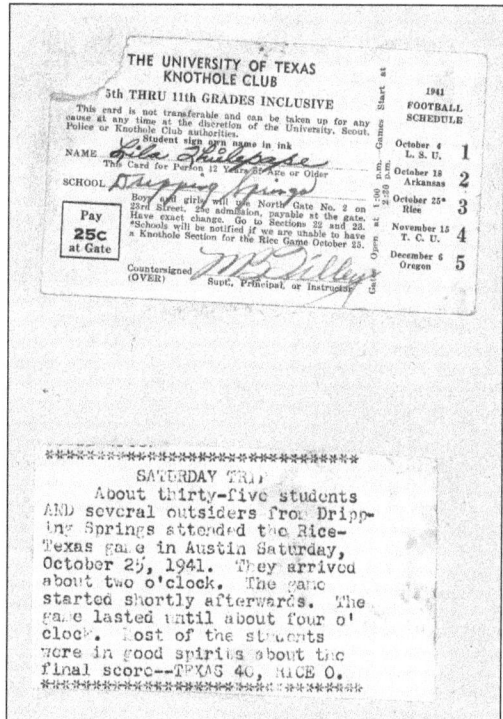

THE UNIVERSITY OF TEXAS
KNOTHOLE CLUB

5th THRU 11th GRADES INCLUSIVE

This card is not transferable and can be taken up for any name at any time at the discretion of the University, Scout Police or Knothole Club authorities.

Student sign his name in ink

NAME *Lila Thielepape*

This Card for Person 12 Years of Age or Older

SCHOOL *Dripping Springs*

Pay 25c at Gate

Boys and girls will use North Gate No. 2 on 23rd Street, 25c admission, payable at the gate. Have exact change. Go to Sections 22 and 23. *Schools will be notified if we are unable to have a Knothole Section for the Rice Game October 25.

Countersigned (OVER)   Supt., Principal, or Instructor

	1941 FOOTBALL SCHEDULE	
October 4	L. S. U.	1
October 18	Arkansas	2
October 25*	Rice	3
November 15	T. C. U.	4
December 6	Oregon	5

SATURDAY TRIP

About thirty-five students AND several outsiders from Dripping Springs attended the Rice-Texas game in Austin Saturday, October 25, 1941. They arrived about two o'clock. The game started shortly afterwards. The game lasted until about four o'clock. Most of the students were in good spirits about the final score—TEXAS 40, RICE 0.

87

Garnett brothers Travis (left) and Billie had a lot to look forward to in Dripping Springs. Their family owned businesses in town, and their futures looked safe and secure. They could not know that World War II was just around the corner and about to yank them out of their sleepy, small-town lives. (Travis Garnett.)

Four

POLITICS

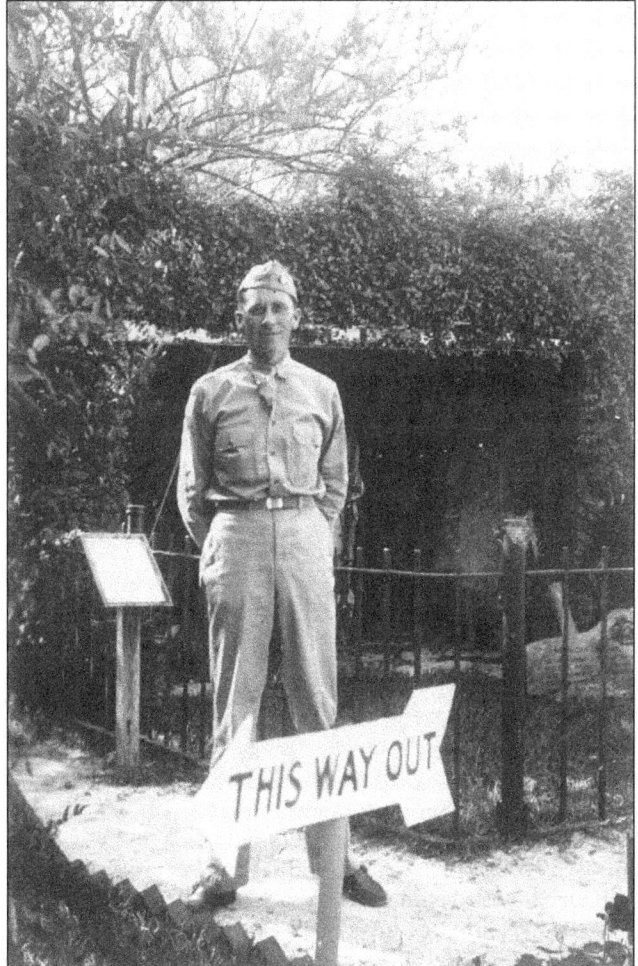

As World War II loomed, the military draft became the way out for many of the area's young men, whether they were looking for one or not. Pictured here is Dripping Springs native D.C. Thielepape, ready to ship out from Florida to serve in Europe in the early 1940s. Thielepape had been working in the Civilian Conservation Corps (CCC)—a New Deal public work-relief program—when Pearl Harbor was attacked. CCC workers were transferred directly into the Texas 36th, which trained several native Dripping Springs boys. (Lila Thielepape Gillespie.)

In 1942, Dripping Springs resident David Crenshaw was stationed in New Mexico, with the Army Air Corps (Air Force). He served in Italy in World War II and later did airborne reconnaissance in Vietnam, before the war was official. Crenshaw was not a lifelong resident of Dripping Springs, although his local family ties go back to the late 1800s. At age 91, Crenshaw remarked about the years he lived in Dripping Springs: "Once you live in Dripping Springs for any amount of time, you'll always say you're from Dripping Springs" (G. B. Mading.)

Travis Garnett was drafted in 1944 and served with the Navy in the Philippines. Garnett is pictured (at bottom left) with his honor guard detail. This detail also buried the dead. Like every boy raised in Hays County, Travis knew his way around guns and was no stranger to burials either. His grandfather William S. Garnett was the town blacksmith in the 1920s and also provided caskets and served as the town funeral director. After the war, Travis carried on the family tradition of multifaceted service to the community back home by serving in the local fire department for 40 years. Later named after him, the Travis Garnett Volunteer Fire Department—which is no longer in operation—was located on the "Triangle," at the intersection of Mercer Street and Ranch Road 12 in Dripping Springs. (Travis Garnett.)

Dripping Springs resident D.C. Thielepape served in Italy and France and was awarded the Bronze Star Medal, an individual military decoration given by the US Armed Forces for acts of bravery, merit, or meritorious service. When awarded for bravery, it is the fourth highest combat award for the armed forces. Sergeant Thielepape is buried at Phillips Cemetery on Ranch Road 12.

John McCarty left Henly with the US Army in 1941 and was sent to the Philippines that same year. McCarty was taken prisoner by the Japanese in the spring of 1942. He survived the Bataan Death March and was marked for death several times during his three-year captivity. McCarty weighed just 76 pounds when he was finally liberated. The town of Henly turned out to give the hometown boy a hero's welcome in 1945. McCarty—pictured in front, on the right—said he survived because of his strong faith in God, his will to live, and the prayers of his mother. He received numerous awards for his service, including two Purple Hearts and two Bronze Stars. (Henly Homecoming.)

The area men who returned from World War II settled down to start contributing to the nation's postwar baby boom. Lifelong Dripping Springs resident Travis Garnett (left) holds his infant son Gary and poses with former classmate Bill Spillar after a snowfall in 1948. (Travis Garnett.)

Like elsewhere in the United States, the pace of the local economy picked up after the war. One of the boons to the Dripping Springs economy was the driving of test cars. Tire manufacturers paid locals to drive cars throughout the Hill Country to test the tires, probably because of the extreme temperatures and miles of winding, hilly roads in the area. Resident Lila Thielepape Gillespie remembers fleets of cars roaming the roads from Dripping Springs to Johnson City. Several gas stations sprang up as paved roads became more common, and additional modern conveniences came to town. The building pictured to the right of this snow-frosted gas station on Mercer Street was the town's movie theater, but not for long. (Travis Garnett.)

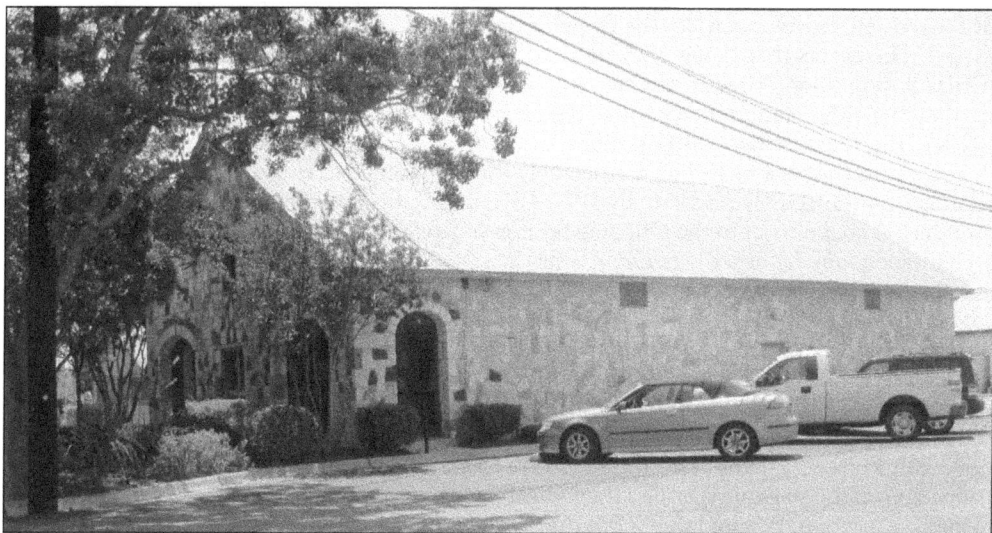

The Crenshaw/Ferrell movie theater was probably a good idea but likely ahead of its time. The town of Dripping Springs was growing, a new highway was coming, and it was still a fairly long trip into Austin for entertainment. Built in 1937 to hold as many as 300 moviegoers, the venture failed by 1940. It was reopened in 1945, showing movies on the weekends. But the theater closed its doors again in 1948. After changing hands and purposes several times over the next few decades, the building finally became a Wells Fargo Bank branch in 2000.

By the early 1950s, it was time for the Dripping Springs schools to enjoy a postwar-boom makeover as well. The events that brought about today's Drippings Springs Independent School District (DSISD) were a long time in the making, from the private Dripping Springs Academy and surrounding, tiny community schools of the late 1800s to the public common schools in the early 1900s to the county school districts and additions of high school grades in the 1920s and 1930s. By the 1940s, the pace picked up considerably through increased consolidation of the common schools into the county districts. By 1950, Dripping Springs voters agreed to convert from a rural high school district to the Dripping Springs Independent School District. This meant state accreditation, among other benefits. About the same time, the Bee Cave District—located to the north in Travis County—was added, increasing the size of the DSISD and making it a two-county district. By 1952, the new DSISD facilities pictured were in place. The modern complex housed grades 1 through 12, as well as the district administration offices, and it included the first cafeteria and gymnasium-auditorium for Dripping Springs students. The dedication of these facilities marked a significant turning point for education in the area, as indicated by the impromptu speech delivered by a young US senator who was recognized in the crowd and personally known by many. This future US president named Lyndon B. Johnson spontaneously jumped up on the stage and thrilled the locals by acknowledging their hard work and dedication to public education. Pictured in front of the new facilities on Easter Sunday 1952 are, from left to right, Avery Wayne Breed, his sister Carolyn Breed, their mother, Irene Combs, and aunt Shirley Combs. (Carolyn Breed Gully.)

Young Peggy Needham, of Dripping Springs, pictured here at age six, was the mascot for the Dripping Springs High School pep squad in 1947. School spirit was high for the enlarging Dripping Springs Independent School District throughout the 1950s and 1960s, but the 1970s brought the biggest challenge area voters and students had faced. An enrollment boom in the 1970s made a new, separate high school facility necessary. By this time, the once sparsely populated Bee Cave District in Travis County—part of the DSISD in Hays County—had grown tremendously through the development of the Lakeway community. Residents on that side of the district did not want to bus their students all the way down to a new facility in Dripping Springs. Naturally, the residents of Dripping Springs did not want their students to travel all the way up to Lakeway. The battle that ensued between the two factions to split the district ultimately lasted 10 years and included several public fights with punches thrown. It was also a clash of two different cultures, and insults were reportedly hurled back and forth, with the Hays County side referred to as "cedar choppers" and the Travis County side referred to as "lake rats." Bonds to build two separate schools failed. Other issues for Hays County voters included water-delivery logistics, fears of rising taxes, and being outgunned on the school board by Lake Travis representation and revenues. The district split was finally approved in court after several years of lawsuits and legal wrangling, and the new Lake Travis Independent School District (LTISD) was born in 1981. But the embers from that bitter battle still smolder on both sides and are reignited each year in Dripping Springs, during the annual football rivalry. (Peggy Needham Montgomery.)

Dripping Springs native Gary Garnett poses in front of a new Tigers scoreboard in the 1950s. Tiger pride in Dripping Springs remains strong, and hope springs eternal as the district continues to grow. The familiar maroon and gold that festoon the town in the fall were not always the DSISD colors, and the mascot was not always a tiger, according to Carl Waits's book *The Complete History of Dripping Springs*. Waits reports the mascot was once a cardinal, and the colors were red and white until about 1938, when someone in the district reportedly got a great deal on maroon-and-gold athletic uniforms that had not been picked up by the organization that originally ordered them. Apparently, a tiger was thought to be more fitting for the new uniforms, and today's Tigers fans can be thankful for a more ferocious mascot to cheer. (Travis Garnett.)

The nearby town of Henly continued to thrive into the early 1950s. The Henly Store and Gas Station on Highway 290 West is pictured doing a brisk business in 1954. (Henly Homecoming.)

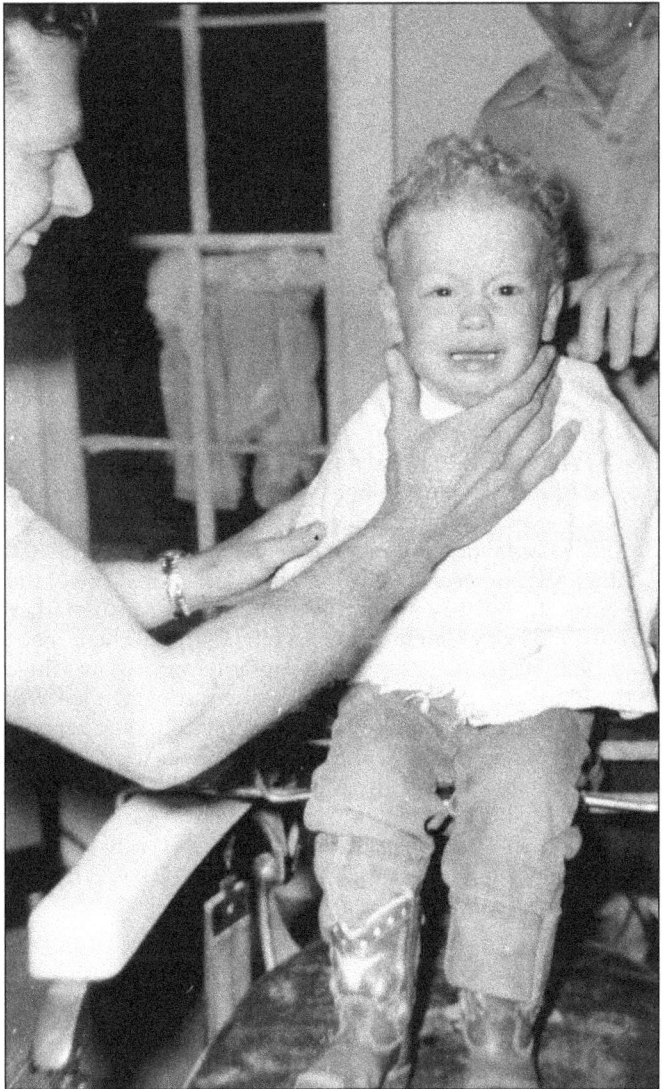

Young Billy Gravenor's first haircut at Lindsey Twidwell's barbershop in Henly may have been a "Kodak moment" for the adults, but it definitely looks like something little Billy would rather forget. Billy's dad, Charles, helps out. (Henly Homecoming.)

The nation was shaken on November 22, 1963, when US president John F. Kennedy was assassinated in Dallas, about four hours north of Dripping Springs by car—which leads to the strange story of Rosco White and the alleged role that Dripping Springs may have played in the assassination plot. According to a diary that White's son Ricky claims to have inherited and read, his father—Rosco, or Roscoe—was part of a three-assassin team. Ricky held a press conference in 1990, sponsored by the JFK Assassination Information Center in Dallas and the Assassination Archives and Research Center in Washington, DC, claiming his father fired two of the six shots that day from where he was allegedly situated on the grassy knoll. White says his father and the other two assassins then fled to a hideout on a ranch in Dripping Springs, where they remained for several days. White claims his father's diary disappeared after he turned over the contents of his father's footlocker to the FBI. Another JFK assassination theorist named Joe West believed the story and went on television in Dallas and Houston, claiming to have a "taped confession" from a "mob hit man from Dripping Springs, TX, known as the 'Black Ace.'" According to West, the Black Ace would talk if given immunity by the government, which apparently did not happen. Rosco White died in 1971, following an explosion and fire while he was working at the M&M Equipment Company in East Dallas. White allegedly told a pastor who visited him several times on his deathbed in the hospital that the explosion was no accident and that White had led a "dangerous double life."

LBJ's rural Central Texas roots shone through much of his Great Society legislation as president, which included support and advancements for education, Medicare and Medicaid, public broadcasting, and environmental protection. Known to be politically domineering and coercive, LBJ most notably advanced civil rights legislation, perhaps demonstrating the kind of community inclusion modeled by his former neighbors in Blanco and Hays Counties with the residents of the freedmen's colonies. President Johnson is pictured signing the Civil Rights Act of 1964, which outlawed discrimination against blacks and women. Dr. Martin Luther King is among those surrounding the president as the bill is signed.

Another twist of fate that tied Dripping Springs residents to the JFK assassination was the elevation of the area's former young senator to the office of the presidency. Vice Pres. Lyndon Baines Johnson, from nearby Johnson City, was sworn in as the 36th president of the United States on the day his predecessor died. LBJ served out JFK's term and was easily reelected in 1965.

The wooden schoolhouse at the freedmen's Peyton Colony, just south of Henly, finally closed in 1963, but not before having indoor bathrooms installed in a cinderblock addition. When the Civil Rights Bill was signed into law by Pres. Lyndon B. Johnson, their former US senator and neighbor, students from Peyton Colony were integrated into the Blanco schools. Among students sent to Blanco were two contemporary Peyton Colony residents, who report they did not experience the violence that plagued schools around the country during desegregation.

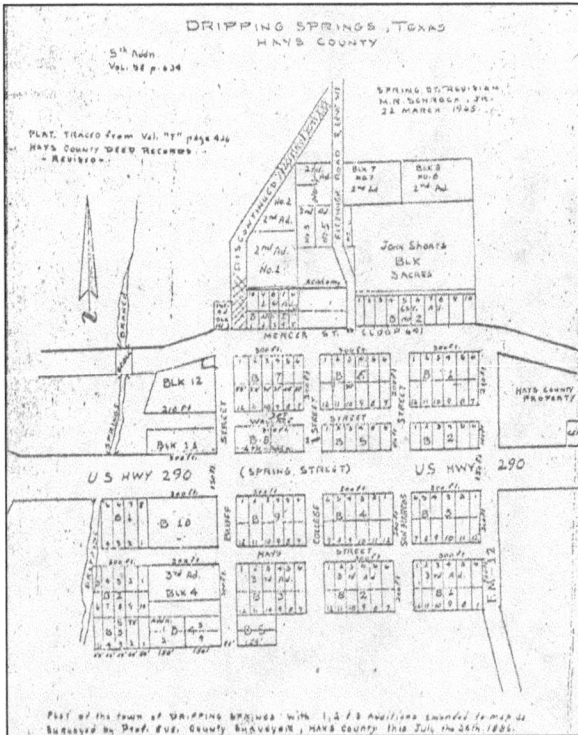

The impact of Highway 290, the so-called superhighway at that time, is clear in this "5th Addition" 1965 map of Dripping Springs, with the Mercer Street "Loop" becoming more of a business-district bypass. Officially referred to as RM (Ranch-to-Market Road) 12 by the Texas Department of Transportation, FM (Farm-to-Market Road) 12 was later extended to its current terminus point at Hamilton Pool Road (RM 3238) in Travis County, six miles west of Bee Cave. (Drane & Associates.)

The town of Henly had been in a slow but steady decline since the end of World War II. By 1966, the post office was closed. Lifelong resident Sally Gravenor recalls, "A new four-lane highway came through. First the garage closed, then the barbershop. A few years later, the post office was gone and then the grocery store. All that is left now are the memories that many of us recall as a happy time when we were young." (Henly Homecoming.)

"Downtown" Driftwood has not changed much over the past century. The town still has its own zip code with a post office in operation. The area is enjoying a slow renaissance as a foodie destination because of a growing number of wineries and eateries opening in the vicinity.

D.S. NEWS
by Margaret Williamson

Charles Tharp and Tommy Williamson attended the Texas-Wyoming football game Sat. night.

Mark Crumley, Tommy Moore and Ricky Gage were involved in a car accident. Fortunately none of the boys were injured.

Chad Murphy received a deep cut on his heel from the slip of a knife.

Janet White was honored with a "farewell" party before she left for South Carolina to join the armed forces.

The Jim Taylors and the Paul Sorrells attended a seminar in San Antonio on Women Who Want to be Women -- ladies you had better take seriously the article you read in the Roadrunner last week on this very thing. (Editor's note: The article referred to was not an article per se. It was a paid advertisement.)

Joe Williamson and Monty McNair are sporting new rings -- their University of Texas graduation rings.

Carl, Susan and Timmy Waits attended the wedding of Carl's youngest brother in Canada, Texas, over the weekend.

The Methodist Church had a covered dish dinner and fellowship this past Sunday at noon.

There will be a covered dish supper at the next civic club meeting Monday, Oct. 21 at 7 p.m. Everyone is invited and urged to join the Civic Club. The meeting will be held in the school cafeteria. You don't have to be a member to attend the supper.

Tracy Johnson was elected Secretary of the FFA in the district. Congratulations Tracy.

There were approximately 35 students who visited Six Flags on Sept. 28. This trip was sponsored by the Baptist Churches and chaperoned by the Tommy Johnsons, Bob and Barbara Burke and others.

There will be a pink and blue baby shower for Kay Hall Blair at the Methodist annex on Tues. Oct. 1 at 8 p.m. Everyone is invited.

Frank Toungate has been moved to the Rebecca Baines Nursing Home in Austin.

Mark Crumley is attending night school at Austin Community College.

Val Sanchez, Denny Williamson, and Russell Burke were injured in the Hays football game. Ricky Lindholm received a sprained ankle in practice. Tommy Moore is almost ready to get back into action. From all reports, everyone will be ready to go at our next game.

Ed and Linda Oliver and boys visited Eddy in Dallas this past weekend.

DRIFT-WOOD NEWS
by Mrs. Wm. Ligon

Driftwood residents haven't been traveling over the country too much these days. However, Mr. & Mrs. Hudson Dildy and Lorena Martin recently enjoyed a vacation in the Ozarks where they visited Hot Springs Eureka Springs. They also spent some time with Hudson's cousin, Mr. & Mrs. Luther McIntarf in Nashville, Arkansas.

Mrs. Vera Collier stayed with her sister, Mrs. Nova Malone, in Pearsall last week.

Mr. & Mrs. Norman Martin and Natalie and Bobby Adkins of Austin visited their mother-in law, Mrs. Lorena Martin last week.

Mrs. Syd Hall returned Sat. from Abilene after a visit with her little grand-daughter, Nicole Hall and mother Betty. Cliff is still in Germany and Betty May.

The Driftwood Volunteer Fire Dept. meets at 7 p.m., Tuesday, Oct. 1.

The October community supper will be held Saturday evening, October 5 at the Driftwood Community Center.

HENLY NEWS
by June McCarty

There was quite a bit of visiting this past week. Allen Halm visited his grandparents, Mr. & Mrs. Wallace of Ft. Worth. Sallie Rust went to Luling with her neices, Enis Follis and Annie Fisher, to attend the 50th Anniversary of another neice and her husband, Mr & Mrs. H. B. Chamness. The reception was held in the club house.

Mr. & Mrs. Robert Wood from Mt. View, Calif., visited with Mr. & Mrs. Gene Smith.

Dr. & Mrs. Leonard Twidwell of Texas City are visiting here this week. They are doing some work on their house while here. Always nice to have them around.

Was good to see Alice McNair in church Sunday. She has really been missed, and we're all happy she's feeling better.

The Chilympiad was a big success. The couldy skies threatened rain all weekend, but luckily it never came. A big crowd attended. It's really something to see. Lynn and I attended the first three days, and enjoyed it very much. There were 114 chili cooks, and all were different. Each had his own theme. I never tasted so many kinds of chili -- some good and some -- well... It was fun anyway. There was lots of activity for all. Louise Gravenor drove her '35 Ford in the parade. It's the second largest in Texas, and was very nice. Plan to attend next year, I think you'll enjoy it.

Was sorry to hear about William Thorpe being burned.

Henly Baptist Church added a new member -- Dale Leidy from Mt. Creek Ranches. We all welcome him.

Mr. & Mrs. Ronald McCarty gave a birthday dinner Sept. 22 for their mothers, Mrs. Chuck Draper and Mrs. Clyde McCarty. Both have birthdays in Sept.

Vira Hester is in Monte Siesta Nursing home. I visited her this week. She's doing much better.

Well, I will close with this thought; "We should be lenient in our judgment, because often the mistakes of others would have been ours had we had the opportunity to make them."

PUBLISHER
D. M. Goeres
Phone; 512-833-4812

CIRCULATION:
Edna Kirkland

EDITORIAL:
Editor: Bruce Crisp

Columnists:
Dripping Springs -
Margaret Williamson
Driftwood -
Mrs. William Ligon
Henly - June McCarty

Writers: Mary Sue Lyle, Jim Taylor, Randy Rogers, Allen Petmecky

ADVERTISING
Bruce Crisp, Mary Hadaway

Despite the closing of the Henly Post Office in the late 1960s and the relative stagnation of the town of Driftwood by the 1970s, the two towns still retained their distinct community identities, as illustrated by this 1974 page from *the Roadrunner* newspaper. Everyone in all three communities knew what everyone else was doing, with whom, and where, thanks in part to the *Roadrunner* stories. Roadrunners, by the way, are large, local ground birds, commonly seen running around Dripping Springs. And, yes, there are also coyotes in the area. (Grady Moore.)

Five

BOOMING AND BLOOMING

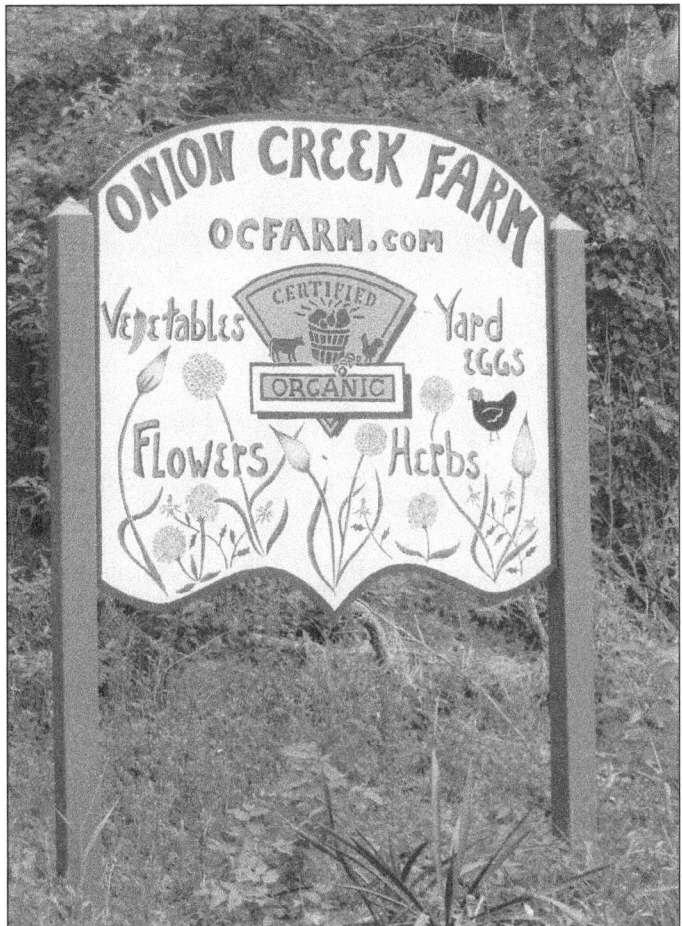

Certified organic by the Texas Department of Agriculture since 1991, Onion Creek Farm sits along the banks of Onion Creek in Dripping Springs. Owner Marianne Simmons is a biologist and former produce manager at the original Whole Foods Market in Austin.

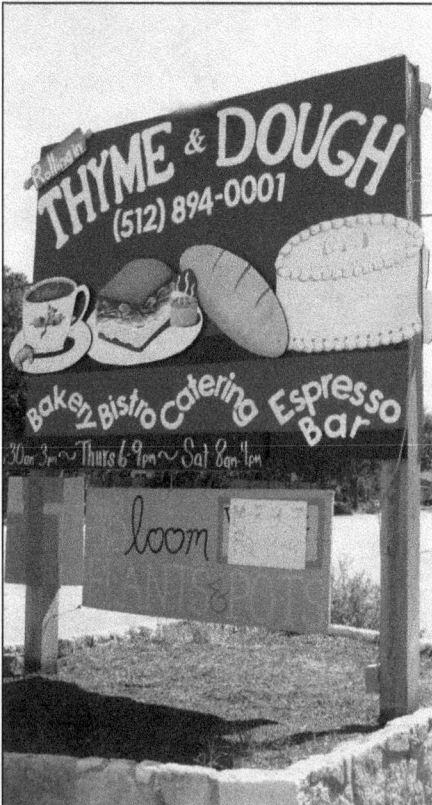

Updating the area's subsistence farming practices of the past, organic farming in the form of market gardens has been making a steady comeback since the 1980s. Onion Creek Farm produces culinary herbs and seasonal vegetables, including garlic, tomatoes, squashes, chilies, and greens. Seen here, the barn fills up in May with bunches of hand-pulled garlic heads and shallots, hand-trimmed and hanging to cure in preparation for the local farmers' market season. Owner Marianne Simmons also sells her boutique botanicals to Austin's Wheatsville Co-op and several other local chefs and restaurants.

Among Onion Creek Farm's best customers in Dripping Springs is the kitschy Rolling in Thyme & Dough café, known around town simply as Thyme & Dough. The bakery-café took over a 100-year-old cottage and surrounded it with a blooming market garden. The resulting experience created for customers by owners Marsha Shortwebb and Fabienne Bollom is a charming and aromatic indoor space, encircled by a visually delightful, shady outdoor space—both areas with tables and wireless connectivity—where locals can meet, eat, work, or just pop in to pick up Euro-styled bakery treats or a new plant for their home garden.

In 2009, the City of Dripping Springs worked with local growers to establish a weekly farmers' market. The market operates from 9:00 a.m. until noon on Saturdays, from May to October, in the shaded Triangle bordered by Highway 290, Mercer Street, and Ranch Road 12. Locally produced salsas, jams, and jellies are sold alongside a variety of produce direct from the farm.

The Pure Luck Farm and Dairy was established on land that once contributed to the Henly area's tomato-producing fame in the 1930s. In 1988, Pure Luck was among the first farms in Texas to apply for organic certification. The farm supplies culinary herbs to grocers and restaurants around Central Texas. Also home to herds of Nubian and Alpine goats since the 1990s, Pure Luck is distinctly associated with artisanal goat cheeses produced solely with milk from resident goats. Private tours of the farmstead include cheese tastings.

AWARD WINNING GOAT CHEESE

★

MADE RIGHT HERE IN DRIPPING SPRINGS!

PURE LUCK

FARM & DAIRY

VISIT US ONLINE AT PURELUCKTEXAS.COM

The Cloud family, from Dripping Springs, checks out an alpaca family from Hummers Homestead at the annual Dripping Springs Founder's Day Festival. Updating the area's historic market for the fleece of locally raised mohair from Angora goats, today's alpaca breeders say their animals are easy to care for and produce a profitable fleece. Melody Moon Farms in Driftwood, another local alpaca breeder, is one of more than a dozen members of the Alpaca Breeders of the Texas Hill Country.

Olives are taking root as an emerging market in the area. In 2011, the family-run organic Texas Hill Country Olive Company was one of just four Texas growers producing olives and US-produced olive oils. Located on Fitzhugh Road, west of Ranch Road 12 in Dripping Springs, its plans include a storehouse and mill house along with a tasting bar, art gallery, restaurant, and olive mill demonstration area.

The New Canaan Farms sign has been a familiar sight on 290 West in Henly for more than 20 years. The store sells homegrown jams, jellies, salsas, and dip mixes, as well as gift boxes and baskets.

Bringing a bit of Italy to Driftwood since 2007, the Mandola vineyards occupy 20 acres above Onion Creek and produce a variety of wines for the Mandola label. Food and wine lovers can sample wine in the on-site tasting room or enjoy a four-course, country-style Italian meal in the Trattoria Lisina restaurant.

From its humble beginnings in this shack at the Camp Ben McCulloch Reunion Grounds, the Salt Lick BBQ has become one of Driftwood's oldest and best-known eateries. The Roberts family first started dishing up barbecue out of the Camp Ben shack in the late 1960s to the descendants of Confederate veterans and their families during their annual summer reunions. Today, the world-famous Salt Lick has been featured nationally and internationally on television and in magazines and has won numerous food awards.

In 1967, Salt Lick founder Thurman Lee Roberts Sr. dug the heel of his boot into the ground to mark the spot where he wanted to build a barbecue pit on his land, directly across from the entrance to the Camp Ben property. Thurman's son Scott and ranch hand Lupe Alvarado built the round pit using stone quarried on the family ranch. Scott and Lupe brought loads of sand and gravel up from Onion Creek to mix for the floor around the pit. Cedars were cut for a roadside table, and the family was in business. The now-famous open pit is still in use and is one of a few of its kind in the Texas Hill Country.

Salt Lick BBQ founder Thurman Roberts was not always in the business of selling barbecue. He and his wife, Hisako, left home each Sunday to spend the week traveling throughout Texas for Thurman's job, building bridges on specialized construction crews. When their son Scott was 16, Hisako urged Thurman to find something else to do that would allow them to spend more time at home. Thurman promptly quit his job and called the family together to make a list of ways they could earn a living. Scott recalls that of the 54 things the family listed on a yellow notepad of ideas, number 14 was selling barbecue. That turned out to be a very lucky number for Thurman, Hisako, and their family. (Thurman Roberts family.)

Using recipes handed down from 1800s' wagon trains and trail drives, the Roberts family started selling pit-smoked brisket, ribs, and sausages to weekend passersby on FM 1826. Local residents predicted failure, but one Driftwood family asked for a picnic table so they could stop and eat. Walls and a roof soon went up to seat more customers. The first section sat 12 people. There was no running water, electricity, or bathrooms. Scott Roberts—wearing glasses in this 1976 image—recalls his father cooking all night on Thursdays, sleeping on a cot, and selling barbecue all weekend. Side dishes were prepared at the Roberts house and brought down to the roadside. A movable wall added space for seating as needed. Expansion on the original building where the pit is still housed finally stopped due to an elm tree that Thurman refused to cut down. (Thurman Roberts family.)

The Salt Lick name originated from what is now a sloping, green field that lies between the Salt Lick complex—seen in the distance—and the events venue on the hill above it that Thurman Roberts later built, called Thurman's Mansion. Before the Salt Lick BBQ or Thurman's Mansion was even a gleam in Thurman's eye, this was a hot, dry cotton field on the family ranch, with rows running up and down the hill. Scott Roberts tells how the children had to hoe a row down, back up, and down again before they could get a drink of water. Near the watering well was a patch of large rocks, which served as a salt lick for livestock. Thurman and Scott later built their barbecue pit near this spot. Much like the salt-lick rocks that once provided essential nutrition for the Roberts' animals, the now legendary Salt Lick has become a watering hole and essential nutrition stop for tens of thousands of visitors.

Nothing says star status like stretch-limousine SUVs. This vehicle is just one of seven parked at the Salt Lick Pavilion to transport a group of California winegrowers on tour. And they are not just here for the barbecue. In 2010, the Salt Lick launched Salt Lick Cellars and has already begun to enjoy some renown for its hot-weather Tempranillo grapes. Growers from across the country and around the world are increasingly attracted to the Texas Hill Country because of a hot, sunny, and relatively dry climate that compares closely to that found in southern Italy.

The picture-perfect Salt Lick vineyard might be mistaken for a vineyard in Napa or Europe. Owner Scott Roberts says the goal is to expand the initial 35–65 acres for the production of estate wines. Roberts's daughter, Maile, runs the Salt Lick wine shop, offering local varieties from area producers, such as McPherson Cellars, Fall Creek, and Driftwood Vineyards. The Salt Lick restaurant remains a cash-only, bring-your-own-bottle establishment. Happily, customers can enjoy the wine they buy at Salt Lick Cellars with the food they order at the barbecue restaurant next door.

This liquor store display case features local wine labels from Sister Creek, Texas Hills, Fall Creek, Duchman, Becker, Llano, and Driftwood Vineyards. Displayed on top are wines from Mandola's and Bell Springs Winery, along with a bottle of Dripping Springs Vodka, which has also gained increasing notoriety, both for its quality and for a local distillery explosion in 2008.

Food and wine are not the only rising stars to call the Dripping Springs area home. Drawn by the area's proximity to Austin and to enjoy the laid-back family lifestyle, television's *Friday Night Lights* star Kyle Chandler moved to the area with his wife and two daughters while starring in the acclaimed television show. Chandler's wife, Kathryn, who became actively involved in efforts to preserve and promote the local history and heritage, has said, "We feel extremely blessed to have found this town." (Kathryn Chandler.)

Local star-sightings have included Matthew McConnaughey, a graduate of the University of Texas at Austin and native son with family in the vicinity. Here, the movie star poses for a picture at the Print Plus copy center in 2005, with owner Pam Owens on the right, and employee Cindy Tudor on the left. (Print Plus.)

Lance Armstrong, seven-time Tour de France winner, has also called Dripping Springs home and has brought the final weekend of his annual Livestrong series to town each fall. In 2010, over 5,000 participants in Livestrong Austin-area weekend events raised more than $3 million for the fight against cancer. According to the Livestrong organization in 2011, the money raised each year "will continue to help cancer survivors live life on their own terms and build and support programs and initiatives to help raise awareness of and improve the lives of the 28 million people living with cancer today." (Kreutz Photography, www.kreutzphotography.com.)

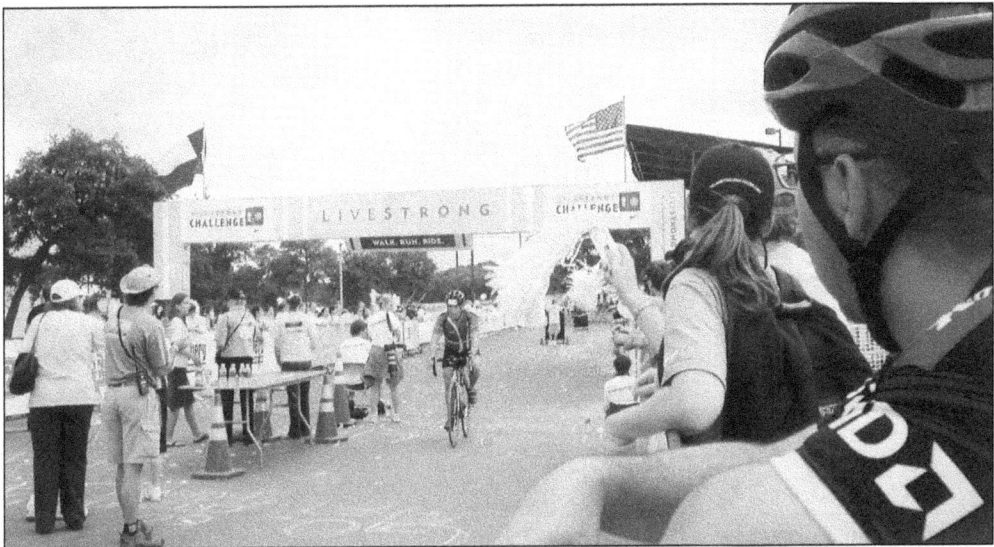

The Livestrong series final ride has taken place in Dripping Springs on Sunday of the Team Livestrong Challenge Austin weekend each year. Multi-distance riders start out from the Dripping Springs Middle School and cover distances from 20 to 90 miles along the area's Hill Country roads. Cyclists definitely outnumber cars on the back roads throughout Dripping Springs, Driftwood, and Henly on that day. (Dripping Springs Chamber of Commerce Visitor's Center.)

Champion barrel racer and Dripping Springs resident Pat Jones has spent a lifetime in the saddle and won numerous rodeo buckles and awards. Her husband, Tom Jones, was a teacher at the Dripping Springs Middle School for 24 years. Tom taught Texas history, geography, and equestrian arts, which included teaching students to shoe horses and rope steers. Pat says she met Tom in a roping pen. Pictured while barrel racing in San Antonio, Pat and her horse amazingly did not knock over the barrel. (Pat H. Jones.)

Aged 78 when this picture was taken, rodeo champion Pat Jones was still riding and teaching her successful barrel racing techniques to young hopefuls, like 13-year-old Olivia Freeman from Dripping Springs. Jones also handcrafts leather saddles in her workshop, visible in the background. Pat says it takes over 50 hours to build a custom saddle, which can cost $2,000 or more, by hand. In 2011, Pat retired from saddle making, but not from passing on her knowledge of saddles, horses, and championship rodeo riding to future generations in the area.

Six

PRESERVING THE PAST

This historic marker tells the story of the freed-slave colony near Henly and is an important reminder of how valuable the history and heritage around Dripping Springs are to the understanding of the area and all of its residents. There are close to 30 Texas State Historical markers across Hays County, with nearly a fourth of those located around Dripping Springs, Driftwood, and Henly. The Dr. Pound Historical Farmstead Museum in Dripping Springs is also a national historic landmark.

Harrison Ranch Park
&
DS Wild West Fest.com

$3,500,000
3,000,000
2,500,000
2,000,000
1,500,000
1,250,000
★1,000,000
★750,000
★500,000
★100,000

Fund Raising Goal
$3,500,000

WILD WEST FEST

Oct. 23rd

GO TEXAN.

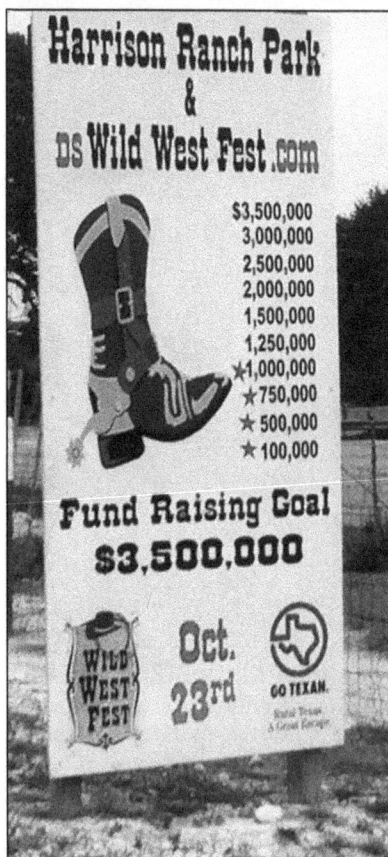

Peyton Colony resident Lawrence Coffee, pictured on the left at age 70, is descended from freed slaves who helped settle the colony. He has learned much of the colony's history orally from older relatives. Coffee was also one of the first African American riders on the Texas rodeo circuit in the late 1960s. He won numerous world titles in roping, despite the professional circuit's prejudice against allowing him to compete. Coffee was finally admitted to the circuit in 1985 and competed across the United States and Canada. He quit rodeoing in 1999 and returned home to Peyton Colony to serve as a deacon at the colony's Mount Horeb church to "keep it going." Many lifelong residents throughout the Dripping Springs area have known Lawrence all his life and continue to join him and the remaining Peyton Colony residents on the church grounds for the annual Juneteenth celebration marking the end of slavery in the United States.

Established in 2008, Harrison Ranch Park in Dripping Springs has 64 acres of woods and open space. The park is operated by the City of Dripping Springs, with a goal to "enable future generations to remain rooted to the hill country lands and rural way of life." Facilities include an outdoor riding arena and over eight acres set aside for wildlife preservation and conservation. Future plans include a wildlife viewing area, riding and hiking trails, and RV and tent campsites.

A young rider competes in a barrel-racing event at Harrison Ranch Park. The event is part of Harrison Ranch's Playday Buckle Series, in which Western riders compete several times between May and October. The final event is run during the park's popular Wild West Fest in the fall, which features competitive rodeo events, food, games, and crafts, all with a Western theme. (Dena McVaney.)

The history of the Texas longhorn is a long and romantic one, from the Old West trail drives through the local area to the herds that can still be seen grazing around Henly, Dripping Springs, and Driftwood. The longhorn is famously associated with Bevo, the mascot for the University of Texas at Austin's football team. Despite the variety of stories about how the mascot got its name, Bevo may simply be derived *beeves*, another word for cattle. Longhorns are sometimes referred to as beeves in journal stories written by residents in the late 1800s about life in the Dripping Springs area. Longhorn populations have been slowly diminishing as open spaces shrink. According to local longhorn owner H.C. Carter, an estimated 20 million head of cattle were driven up the trails from Mexico to Canada from 1865 to 1897.

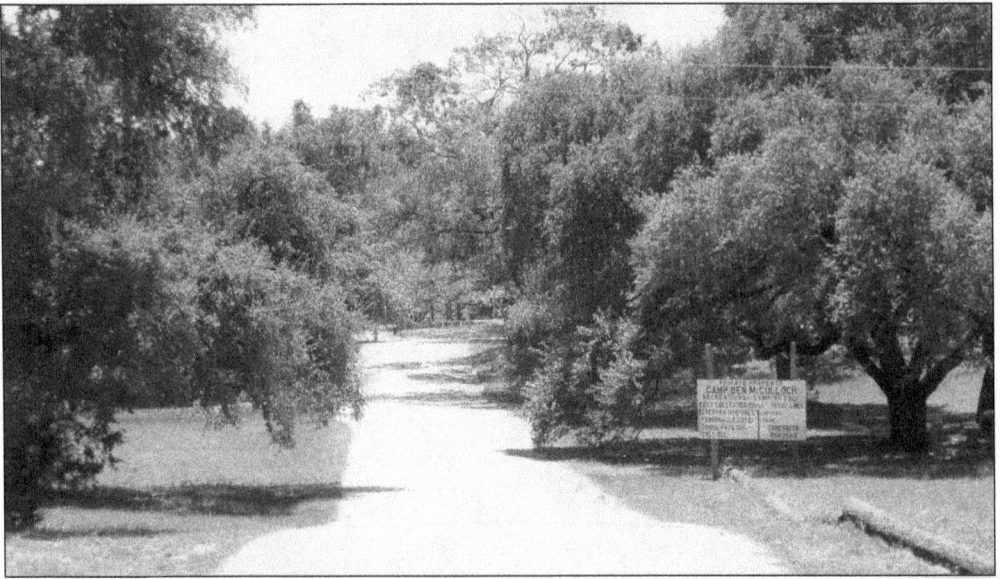

In 2011, Driftwood's annual Camp Ben Reunion marked 115 years. This eight-day celebration includes live music, dancing, camping, swimming, food, and games on the banks of historic Onion Creek. Campsites for descendants of Confederate veterans are reserved year-round with wooden signs, painted with family names and nailed to tree trunks, designating the sites.

Dripping Springs' original Methodist church was built here in 1880, on land deeded to the church by early residents John and Nancy Phillips. Subsequently, members who passed away were buried in the churchyard in customary fashion. The first known grave in Phillips Cemetery is that of B.G. Sorrell, whose grave is surrounded by raised stone walls on all four sides. Because of the hard, rocky ground, early graves were shallow, so stone walls were erected around them to keep out wild animals and help prevent soil erosion from exposing the grave. When the Methodist church building was sold and moved in 1901, the land continued to be used as a burial ground and was finally donated to the community by the church in 1940. Phillips has been maintained by a cemetery association since 1962.

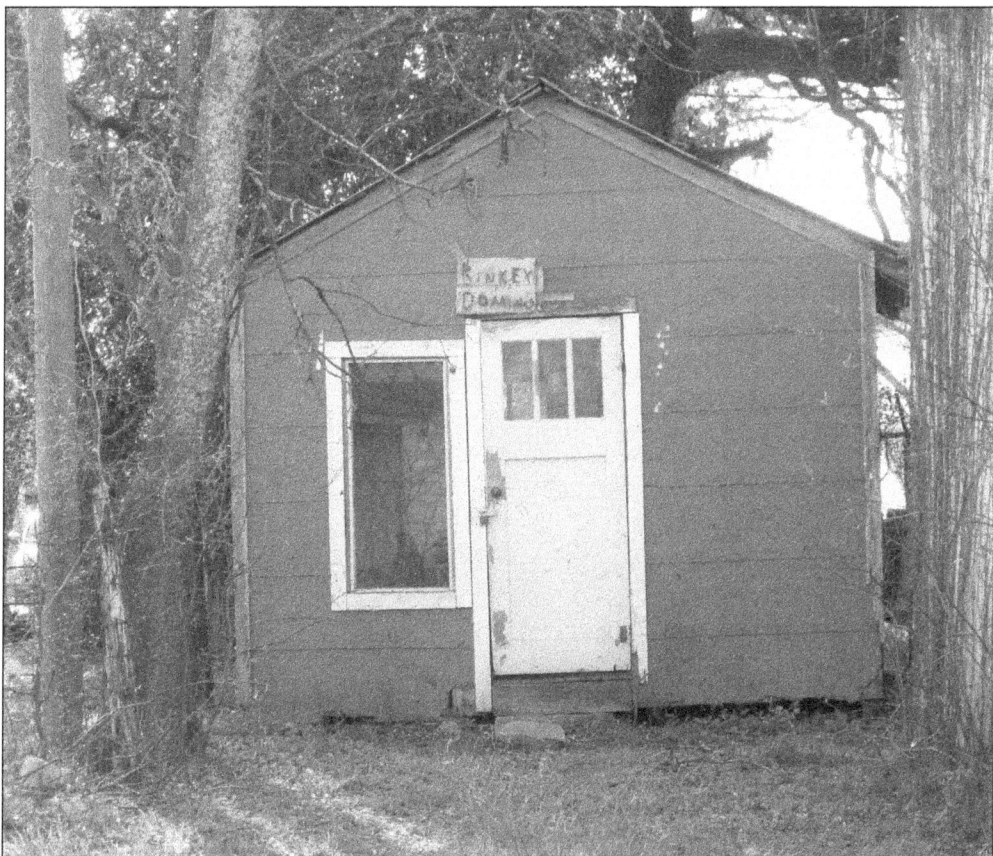

Dominos is a tradition throughout the Dripping Springs area. The game was played so frequently by men in the area that a small shed—generously called a hall—was built in 1939 using proceeds from players who ponied up 25¢ a play. The gaming shack was moved to a less conspicuous location off Mercer Street because the activity was considered gambling.

Anyone who has ever called Henly home is invited to the annual Henly Homecoming. The first homecoming was held in June 1957 on the Twidwell ranch. Multigenerational families—like the Gravenors, pictured—gather each year to enjoy a meal together, tell stories, and pass down their fondest memories of Henly life to the younger generations who still attend.

The annual Fall Fest event, on the grounds of the Dr. Pound Historical Farmstead Museum at Founder's Park in Dripping Springs, has grown into a lively educational experience for young and old. Kids can visit a one-room schoolhouse or dress up as pioneers at Sarah's Closet costume rental. Costumed craftsmen demonstrate 19th-century skills like blacksmithing, spinning, and soap-making. Fiddlers play heritage music under the shade of old live oak trees while visitors chow down on barbecue, homemade pound cake, and kettle corn. All proceeds are used for the ongoing restoration and maintenance of the 1850s historic site. (Dr. Pound Historical Farmstead.)

This Dripping Springs Middle School cheerleader demonstrates how to make a corn husk doll at the 2010 Fall Fest. Other kid-friendly pioneer activities include shooting marbles, rolling hoops, and dipping candles.

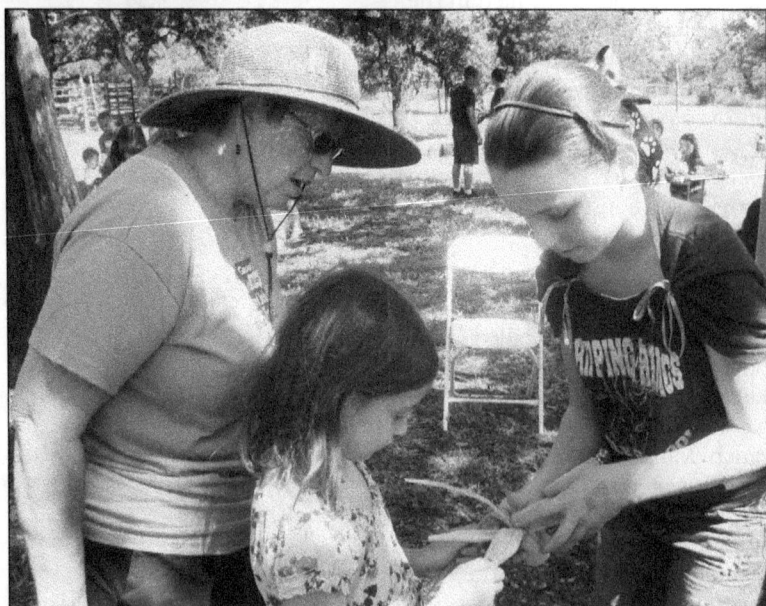

Docents in period dress are available for guided tours of the 1850s dogtrot-style, log pen cabin and historic grounds at the Dr. Pound Historical Farmstead Museum. The museum is located at Founders Park on Ranch Road 12, north of the Highway 290 intersection.

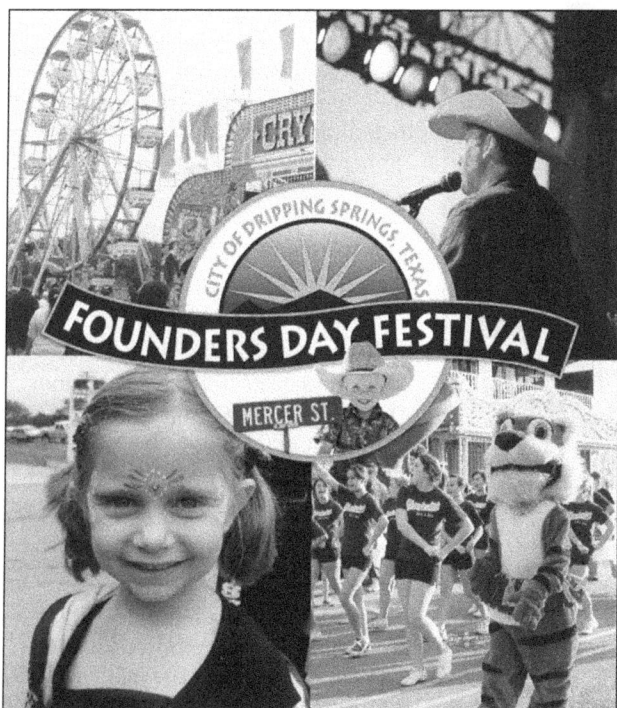

The annual Founder's Day Festival stretches from end-to-end on downtown Mercer Street for an entire weekend. The festival kicks off with a grand parade and features a carnival, live music, vendor booths, and a fiercely competitive barbecue cook-off. The family event was created to commemorate and celebrate the founding families of Dripping Springs. (Pun Nio, NioGraphics, Inc.)

The Dripping Springs Chamber of Commerce Visitors Center is a hub of information about the local history and heritage for visitors and newcomers to the area. Books and brochures are available, including a *Discover Dripping Springs* walking-tour guide.

William Thomas "W.T." Chapman was a newcomer to Dripping Springs in the 1870s. Soon after his arrival, Chapman wed the Marshall widow, who had inherited her late husband's property. This charming old well in front of the historic Marshall-Chapman house—now a bed and breakfast on Mercer Street across from city hall—is a reminder that issues surrounding resources, like water, will be among the many factors that shape the area's future growth.

Seven

FACING THE FUTURE

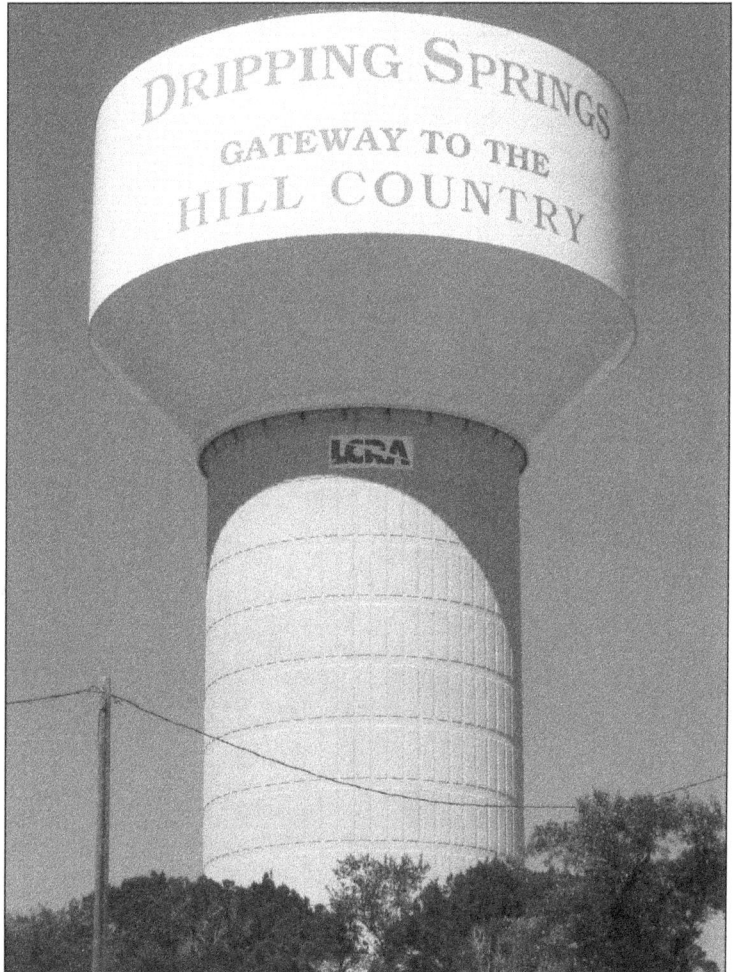

This landmark water tower serves as a daily reminder that continued growth will require effective water management solutions. The widespread removal of groundwater-depleting cedar trees throughout the area may be one highly effective, low-cost solution to help replenish the area's underground water supply.

Other local landmarks visible on the horizon while driving into Dripping include the friendly, familiar steeple of the First Baptist Church—rebuilt after being destroyed by fire in 2007—and the old Dripping Springs clock on the northwest corner of Highway 290 at Ranch Road 12. The sight of this rush hour on an ordinary weekday afternoon in 2011 would have been unimaginable just a year or two earlier.

At the east edge of town on Highway 290, the Nutty Brown Cafe & Amphitheater, better known as the Nut, embodies both the Austin and Hill Country lifestyles as a popular outdoor live-music venue and Tex-Mex family restaurant. Before the doors opened in 2003, the location was already famous as Nutty Brown Mills, known throughout Texas for pralines, a desert still sold at the restaurant.

124

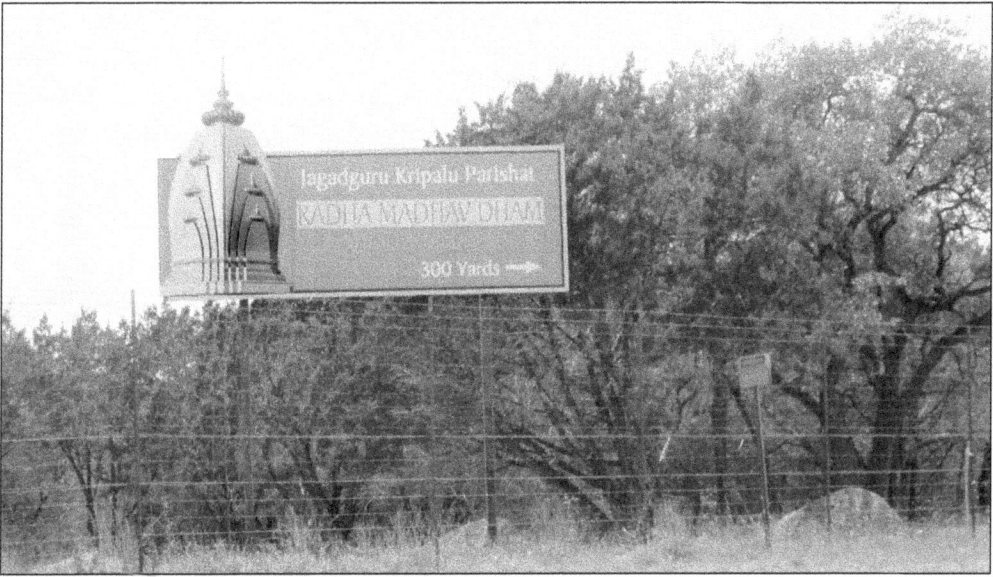

The former location of the historic Friday Mountain Boys Camp is now occupied by a Hindu temple complex that claims to be the largest in the United States. The future of the Hindu site came into question when the 82-year-old Indian guru who established and led the organization for 20 years—Prakashanand Saraswati—was convicted in 2011 of indecent behavior. Now renamed Radha Madhav Dham, the complex hosts celebrations of all major Hindu festivals and promotes cultural awareness.

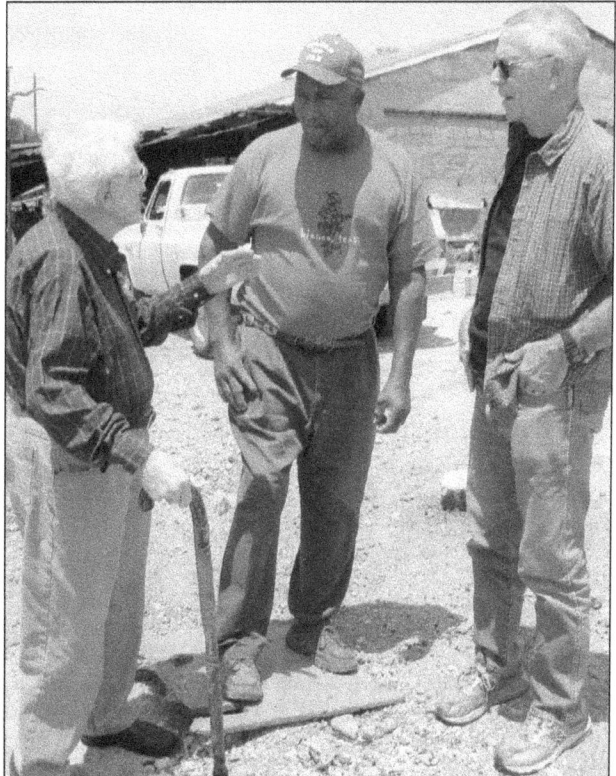

Facing the future also means helping to heal the wounds of history between these former area residents whose ancestors lived on opposite sides of the color divide. In his early 90s in this photograph, former Dripping Springs resident David Crenshaw (with cane) is a descendant of the McQueens, a slave-owning family from Alabama. Traveling with his cousin George B. Mading (right), the pair headed out to Peyton Colony to meet Lawrence Coffee, a descendant of area freed slaves, to learn whether Coffee had any knowledge of what became of three of the former McQueen family slaves after they were emancipated. That information was not known, but the pair learned from Coffee that the Blanco County Library would be one of their best resources to research this information.

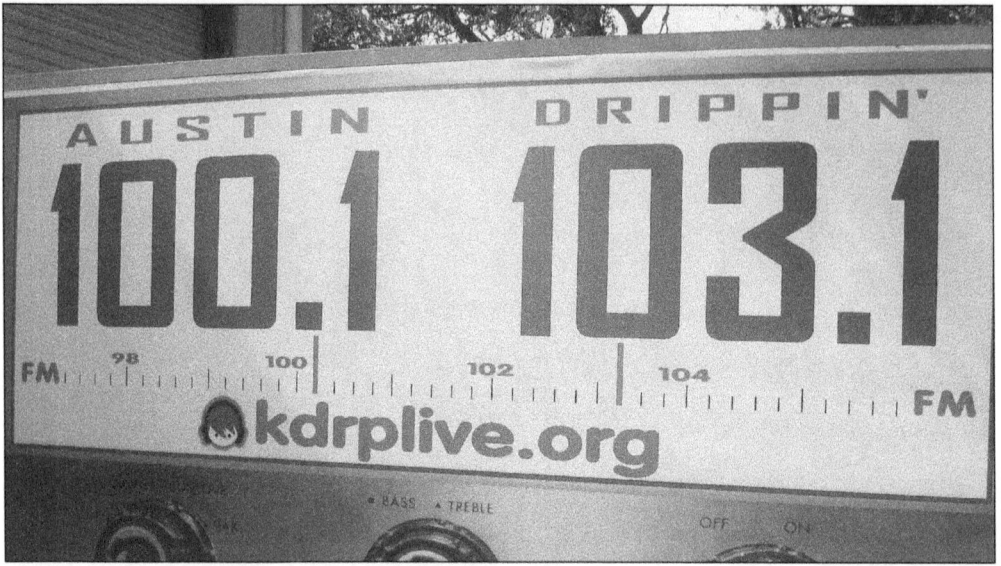

Whatever the future holds, good communication and accurate information will be keys to healthy growth. In a sign of the times, the rapidly changing Dripping Springs area got its own radio station in 2010. KDRP was also adopted as the official radio station of the City of Dripping Springs.

The original Methodist congregation of Dripping Springs met in the one-room log home of Dr. Joseph Pound, beginning in 1854. The first sanctuary was built in 1880, on the site where Phillips Cemetery now stands. Today's sanctuary is located on Ranch Road 12, north of Highway 290, and remains the home of a thriving congregation, built on a legacy of faith for the future.

Mercer Street has been the main street in Dripping Springs since W.T. Chapman laid out the town in 1881. The street was named after his son Mercer. Just one block over from traffic buildups on Highway 290, Mercer Street is still sleepy in 2011—no doubt, not for long.

The 360-degree camera housed in the red ball on top of this Google Maps car rotates to capture digital images while the driver repeatedly crisscrosses area roads. With the car parked near the historic icon of the original Dripping Springs Academy, this 2011 photograph confirms that Dripping Springs and the surrounding areas are "on the map" for the future of Central Texas and the Hill Country.

Visit us at
arcadiapublishing.com